SPRINGFIELD TORNADO

STORIES FROM THE HEART

Shawn Morse & Loretta Kapinos

First Published by AuthorMike Ink, 06/01/2012

www.AuthorMikeInk.com

AuthorMike Ink and its logo are trademarked by *AuthorMike Ink.*

Printed in the United States of America

Book cover design and layout by Enve Creative LLC.

This book is to honor those who lost their lives on June 1, 2011 in the Springfield Tornado:

Angelica Guerrero, 39, of West Springfield
Sergey Livchin, 23, of West Springfield
Virginia "Ginger" Darlow, 52, of Palmer

INTRODUCTION

Shawn Morse
WEST SPRINGFIELD

After witnessing the damage and the heartfelt loss of the June 1st tornadoes, I had to do something. I asked myself: What can one person do to help out his community and surrounding towns? Facebook has so many members. Maybe that way, I can get the word out that people need help.

I created a friend page—Springfield Tornado. Via that route, I asked for photos of the damage and posted them, along with updates. I also encouraged potential observers to stay home and out of the way of EMS and cleanup crews. The idea was to assist with a more rapid clean up and prevent someone from getting hurt or killed by falling debris.

Once I started posting photos, my Springfield Tornado Facebook page grew fast—5000 friends worldwide in

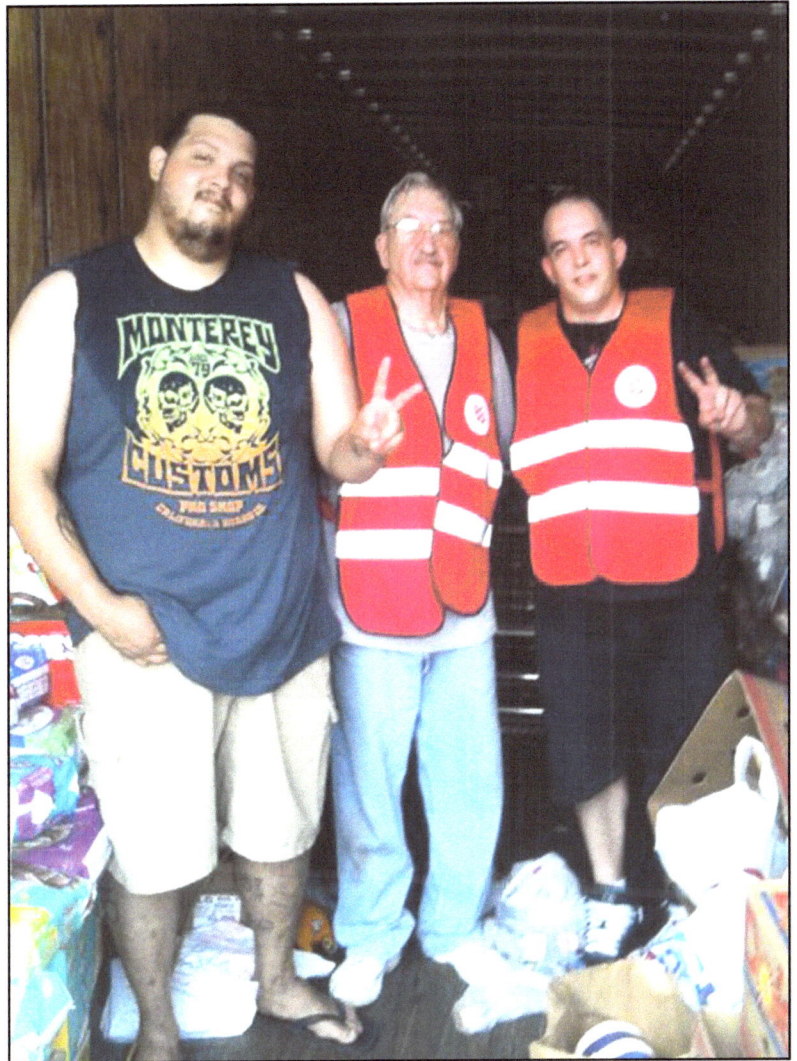

just three days. I asked the members of Springfield Tornado to spread the word to those affected. Tornado victims could be given a voice by posting what exactly they needed. I struggled to keep up with the demand for help. I spent countless hours trying to direct aid to those who needed it most. My girlfriend, Tisha, filled in, too. During that time, Big Y in West Springfield held their food drive. I helped out, loading the truck and taking donations. I worked beside some of the greatest people I will ever meet—loving people with big hearts.

In late summer, I asked for tornado victims to send in their stories. I posted a desire for a publisher to create a book, so I could donate a portion of the proceeds to tornado victims and disaster relief. I received a message from Loretta Kapinos expressing an ability to help. My prayers were answered.

Almost one year post June 1st tornadoes, I am still managing Springfield Tornado. My goal is to turn Springfield Tornado into a national, nonprofit tornado relief foundation. Springfield Tornado keeps growing: three Facebook pages, a Youtube channel, Myspace profile, Twitter page, and website www.SpringfieldTornados.com. We have two messaging systems as well as two e-mails. I hope Springfield Tornado can help tornado victims all across the United States for years to come.

Catherine Reynolds
LUDLOW

June 1, 2011 is a day I'll never forget. I was in Ludlow Massachusetts, coaching the Ludlow Varsity Cheerleading team for tryouts, just outside the high school. I had an awful feeling. Maybe that's why I broke my own rule and answered my cell phone during practice. It was my boyfriend, Eric, informing me of a tornado that touched down in Springfield. It was moving right toward us, in Ludlow.

It took me a minute to actually process what he said. When I finally realized what was happening, I told the girls to pack up and get to the lowest part of the school. In the meantime, I called my mother, Susan, at our home in East Longmeadow. Thankfully, she was already heading toward the basement with our pets.

The girls and I sat in a hallway in the lower level of the school. It has no windows, so I kept running back and fourth to the gym to check the weather. At one point, the outside looked very green and musty. It was also down pouring. On the inside, I felt very nervous, but as a coach I had to keep calm. The girls kept very quiet. Each one called their parents. Some parents came right away. Some came as quickly as they could. I stayed until each of the girls were picked up and then proceeded home myself.

I entered Springfield right near Western New England College. A man pulled up next to me at a light. His car had leaves and dents all over it. He seemed frazzled and asked if I had any cell phone service, as he did not and needed to call home. I asked him if he was okay. That's when he told me he was on the bridge that the tornado crossed over. The winds turned his car around multiple times. Still, despite, his state of shock and the damage to his car, it didn't occur to me that a tornado actually happened.

Normally, it takes me twenty to thirty minutes to get home from Ludlow High. But on June 1st, every way I attempted to travel, downed trees and power lines blocked my way. After two hours of trying, I was not able to get there at all. The radio stations warned of another storm and urged everyone to seek shelter.

My phone was about to die. I couldn't get home. And now another storm. I was scared, but had no idea how bad the situation really was. The nearest place for me to seek a charge and shelter was Sofia's Sports Bar. I stayed there for a while, making new acquaintances until I saw my friend Sam outside. She was on her way across the street to Paddy's Sports Bar. I knew more people there, so I went with her.

My uncle lives in Hampden. He tried to come and get me, but was unable to do so for the same reasons I couldn't get home. Even my boyfriend and his friend drove for hours only to find every street closed. Knowing I was scared, my boyfriend walked through the damage to me around ten-thirty. We stayed at Paddy's until it closed. Finally, we were able to drive to our friend's neighborhood. It was then I saw the extent of what happened.

The tornado hit less than half a mile from my house. Many of my friends' homes were damaged. Thankfully, mine was not.

Two days later, I heard about four cheerleaders who'd lost their homes, I knew we, the cheer team, had to do something. After tryouts, we gathered bottled water and food and headed to Monson. All day, the girls walked and offered contributions to survivors. They donated the rest to a local church for anyone they could not reach. In those moments, the girls realized how lucky they were.

One of my girls even called her father during our mission just to say she loved him.

A few weeks later, the Ludlow cheerleaders went to the Mass Mutual Center in Springfield to cheer up the children and families in the shelter. They passed out pizza donated by the Ludlow

Cheerleading and Booster club and danced with the children. It was so touching to see the smiles of little children while they held hands with varsity cheerleaders.

To this day it breaks my heart to see the areas that were affected and know how blessed my family has been.

Crystal Bell-Everett
SPRINGFIELD, MA

A few coworkers and I stayed late at our office in the South End of Springfield. I was in my boss's office when I felt my ears pop. We all looked at each other with confused expressions. We opened the door to his office and saw a scene out of the Wizard of Oz or as others described "the inside of a big blender."

We relocated to the next office. Behind the closed door, we could hear glass shattering and the sound of a freight train. Thirty seconds later, it was over. We'd only had a two-second warning.

Sure, there'd been tornado warnings earlier in the day, but no one had taken them seriously. We laughed it off. It would never happen here.

Everyone left the office at that time, except me. I called my husband and told him a tornado just hit my work and to take shelter. He said okay and hung up the phone. He didn't believe me.

Everyone was safe, but now we had to evacuate the building. All I can remember about leaving the office was walking on glass. I couldn't believe what I saw once outside. The apartment building to my left no longer had a roof. Most of the trees in front of our building were either uprooted or split in half. Farther down, in the second parking lot, I saw my truck under multiple trees. All I could see was one headlight. In that moment, I thanked God I wasn't inside it when the tornado happened.

I called my husband to come and get me.

He asked, "Why?"

I told him about the trees.

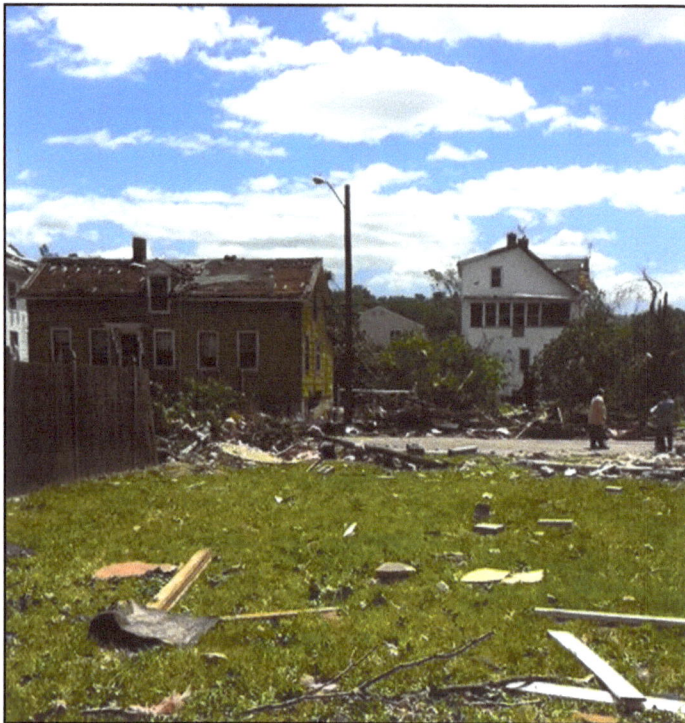

"How did that happen?" he replied.

I asked if he had the news on.

He apologized and said he was on his way.

At that time, we were approved to go back into the building since there was no fire or structural damage. When the warning of a second tornado was announced, people from the community came to us for shelter.

The second tornado warning expired. It was then I tried calling my aunt who lived four streets away from my work. I couldn't get through, but received permission to leave

work to check on her if I brought a companion for safety.

That's when my adventure began.

People were walking all over the South End of Springfield. I practically grew up here in my Grandmother's house. Although it's no longer in my family, it broke my heart to see it crushed under the roof of another building. I saw houses destroyed, people standing in doorways or outside crying, unable to believe what had happened. I can't find words to describe how everyone felt. All I can say is: you can only know if it happens to you.

A police officer stopped me on Wilcox Street. He told me I couldn't go any further due to a gas leak. The last thing I wanted was to give him a hard time, but I was going no matter what. I gave him my name, where I came from, where I was going and explained how I couldn't get a hold of my aunt. He let me through with a warning to watch out for power lines and fallen trees. In retrospect, I wish I'd gotten his name so I could thank him.

As I approached my aunt's house, the damage wasn't too bad. I could do nothing but thank God. My aunt had already heard from my mother who was also okay. My husband made multiple attempts to reach me on my cell, but couldn't get through due to overloaded circuits. He also tried to get to me physically, either by driving or walking, but the police wouldn't let him pass, because he'd already made contact once and knew I was safe.

I sent my husband away at that time. But shortly after, another tornado warning was announced. This time it was close to where I live. Again, I couldn't reach my husband by phone, so I resorted to texting him to advise him to find shelter. I also called my mother who was watching my daughter. My mother cannot go up or down stairs, but she told my daughter to get in the basement. I instructed her to get to the center of the house. At that moment, the line broke up and went dead.

I tried my husband again, but was still unable to reach him. Inside, I was no longer calm, but I forced myself to hold it together for my aunt as I tracked the tornado's location on television.

My only thought was that it wasn't far from my house.

After what seemed forever, I finally got a hold of my mother and daughter. They were safe. The house wasn't hit. Still, it was a while before I heard back from my husband. When he called, he told me he was safe. I've never thanked God so much.

I had to get back to work. This time, I went back via Main Street, where I saw even more damage. People were wandering, searching for loved ones. Most were shaking their heads in disbelief. On Williams Street, I got a better look at what used to be my Grandmother's house. It had been in our family since she immigrated here, until a few years ago. The neighboring roof had crushed the second floor and moved the house a few inches off the foundation. I stopped a moment to hope whoever lived there got out.

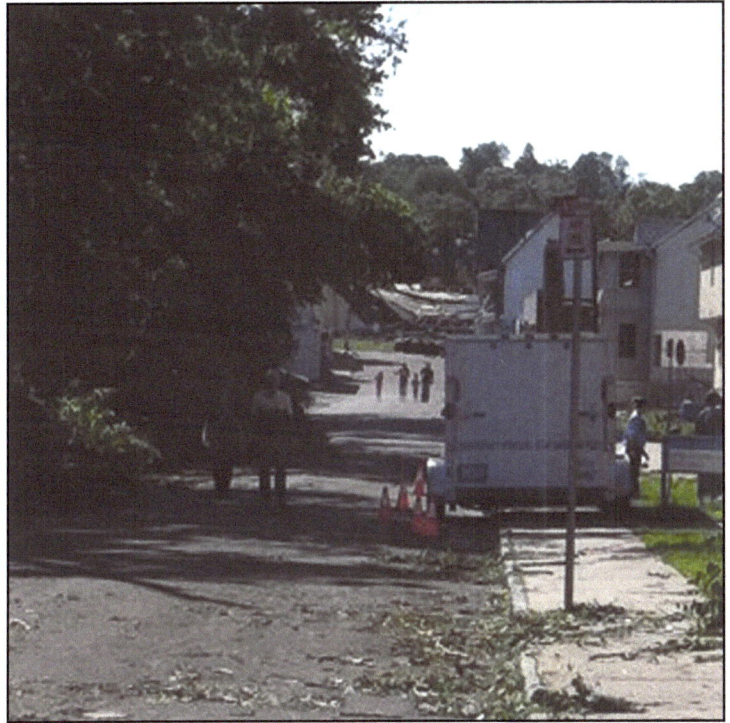

Everyone was busy at work when I arrived. They were trying to help the community by taking in pets for shelter. I spotted someone who came to help who was leaving and headed near my home. Thankfully, they were kind enough to bring me to see my family.

My husband waited for me in the driveway, in the pouring rain.

That night, I received countless texts and phone calls from family and friends. I tried to sleep, but couldn't. Finally, I went back to work at six a.m. to help out in any way I could. I met a lot of people I'll never forget. My husband came with me to help with outside cleanup.

It wasn't until Saturday, a few days later, when I finally stopped. I think my adrenaline wore off. I reflected on what I went through, how lucky I was and how wonderful my work treated our community and me. For a month, I was jumpy when we had wind or a thunderstorm. It took some time for me to get rid of survivor's guilt.

I will never forget June 1, 2011.

What can happen?" Deborah Provost asked herself when she agreed to assume the role of administrator on call the week of June 1, 2011. Traditionally, it's the winter weather that causes disasters. Summer weather in New England was nothing to fear. Or so she thought.

The first page came in while Deborah was in a meeting. The manager at the Orthopedic Surgery Center on Carew Street in Springfield was concerned about a tornado warning she'd heard. She wondered if the patients needed to be pulled out of surgery. Deborah's response was no, for two reasons. First, tornados do not touch down in New England; second, the operating rooms had no windows, so they'd be safe if one did occur.

Deborah returned to her meeting with no further thoughts until the next page came in. The charge nurse in the Emergency Department informed her that a tornado had in fact touched down in West Springfield. At this point, Deborah realized that the Orthopedic Surgery Center was in danger. She called the manager back, instructed her to move all patients to the center of the building and keep all staff in the building. She cancelled her current meeting, as she knew she needed to open the Incident Command Center.

At four-thirty p.m., the Chicopee-Agawam Room, a conference area attached to the cafeteria, opened as the Incident Command Center. Phone banks, the hospital bed tracking system and patient disaster tracking barcode packs were set up. Deborah, as the Incident Commander, assigned tasks and jobs.

The next step was to co-ordinate disaster response with the City of Springfield. Within fifteen minutes, the Springfield Fire Department had their disaster center set up. Baystate Medical Center designated a liaison to that center to facilitate communications between the two.

Deborah then began her large scale survey of the area. Baystate Health System (BHS) includes Baystate Franklin Hospital in Greenfield, Baystate Mary Lane Hospital in Ware and multiple other clinics and facilities. Thankfully, the tornado had diverted away from all BHS owned buildings.

In addition to a rapid facilities assessment, Baystate Medical Center's disaster response requires a survey of all surrounding post-acute facilities: rehab, nursing homes, long term care hospitals. Did other they sustain damage or suffer injuries? Were there power outages that put chronically ill people at risk? Did any facility need to evacuate or send patients to the Emergency Department for help?

With the exception of sporadic power outages and blocked access points, luckily on June 1st, all external facilities were fine.

At 5:02p.m., Baystate Medical Center activated a "Plan D Standby." This is a high alert protocol that involves all staff at Baystate. Everyone must be ready to work where needed, should it be required. And it was clear, staff would be needed. Reports of destruction were coming in via Coordinated Medical Emergency Direction (CMED/the ambulance call system) and other resources. Baystate Medical Center could expect significant injuries.

 Walk-in patients began to arrive just as the Plan was called.

The emergency and trauma teams immediately organized for a surge in activity. Alternate trauma rooms were prepared, as well as family support rooms and places for staff to sleep, should that become necessary. Equipment, resources, services and supplies were mobilized. And per Deborah's direction, an alternate triage was established outside the Emergency Department to prevent the ED from being inundated with both injured patients and the walking well. This last step was taken as a direct lesson from the tragedy in Joplin, Missouri.

At 5:25 p.m., Plan D Standby was promoted to Plan D Active. The hospital and all of its affiliates were to act according to the Disaster Plan Policy.

The next step required Deborah to assess the Emergency Department. How many patients were currently in the Department? Were they admissions or discharges? If they were discharges, did they have some place to go and could they even get there? How many staff members were working at the moment? And who would be available for extended relief? Her priority was not only to keep patients safe, but assist and protect the staff as well.

Finally, communication was established with the city's contracted Emergency Medical Service to plan how they would be utilized. Springfield officials designated The Visiting Nurse Association building on Maple Street as the EMS dispatching area. Its location at the top of the hill, above the area of damage, proved to be an ideal location for triaging patients during the search and rescue.

At 5:30 p.m., a second alert for tornado activity in the area was posted. ALL patients needed to be moved away from windows, into the center of the building. All forms of transportation, including staff shuttles and EMS were required to cease and take cover until further notice. Having never prepared for a tornado, this was a time of very high tension. But eventually the danger passed, and no further damage occurred.

Over the next couple of hours, patients were evaluated and treated. By 7:30 p.m., a few were ready for discharge. An area was created for them to move them out of the ED, but some had no place to go; their homes had been destroyed. This led to a moment of realization for Deborah, the leaders and staff on hand. This disaster was like no other before. It affected the whole community with long reaching consequences. Baystate's shuttle service remobilized and a patient transportation service was created to take victims to the Mass Mutual Center shelter, and Baystate Health Ambulance provided liquid oxygen to those in need.

Another tornado warning was issued around 8:00 p.m. The location was cited right over Baystate Medical Center and Chicopee. Again, all patients had to be moved away from windows. The sky turned black. It appeared the hospital could take a direct hit. Baystate had never drilled employees for a tornado before. All Deborah could do was hope everything would be okay—for her staff, the patients and her family at home. Mercifully, the storm passed.

During this time, Deborah was faced with a situation different from what she ever had to prepare for during a drill. Baystate Franklin Medical Center contacted her to approve the transfer of a heart attack patient, known as a STEMI in medical terms. This type of patient requires a cardiac catheterization, a procedure only specialized hospitals such as Baystate can perform. The alternatives to Baystate are quite a distance away, putting the patient at risk and adding additional stress on the family. The best option for everyone was to send the patient to Springfield. Deborah wondered, could that happen during a disaster?

Deborah knew the hospital could accommodate the patient, but she didn't know if the roads were clear enough for the patient to be transported safely. That's when technology really made a difference. A team member stepped up with an application on his cell phone to see if the route from Greenfield to Springfield was clear. And it was. The patient was transported to Baystate Medical Center for his cardiac catheterization.

Events slowed down around 9:30 p.m. The Command Center stayed open until the next morning, in case more casualties were discovered during the overnight search and rescue efforts. Fortunately, no more patients related to the tornado came in that night.

In retrospect, Springfield had fared well in terms of personal injury. Approximately twenty-five victims were seen and treated at Baystate Medical Center's Emergency Department—a small number in comparison to the overall population of Western Massachusetts. Much speculation has gone into how Western Mass got so "lucky," considering our warning system is not equipped for such events as a tornado. Few solid answers have been found. Maybe it was the hour of day the tornado occurred. Five o'clock is a time for commuting, so many people weren't home. Or maybe it was technology. Our world is connected, up to date via computers and cell phones and that's what saved lives. Possibly, it was the existence of basements in the area. Springfield might not see tornados frequently, but at least it has some places safe to go when needed. No matter what though, the Disaster Team at Baystate Medical Center remains thankful to this day that the number of casualties stayed low.

The Springfield Tornado on June 1, 2011 was not a disaster anyone planned on having but with preparation, even this most unexpected of events was handled professionally, safely and with the utmost of care. The hospital and community continue to review the event, learn from it and use it to plan for the future.

Debra Bouley
SOUTHBRIDGE

I woke up on June 1, 2011 feeling scared. Something was wrong, but I had no idea what it could be. I watched the weather and saw storms were coming. I kept an eye out as I normally would while caring for my two children, Jennifer, nine and Landen, five, and a third boy, almost three.

At about 3:30 p.m., the kids were playing in a kiddie pool. I checked the weather report and radar only to notice thunderstorms moving into our state. I watched the redness grow darker and darker on the screen. I put all three kids in the basement, telling them to "play where it was much cooler." It was now four o'clock.

I heard about the tornado warning shortly after and hurried to share the information with my boyfriend, Jon, and his grandmother, Cathy. They quickly moved around the yard, putting away or tying up every loose object they could find. They also moved our cars around.

At 4:15, I called the three-year-old boy's father with my concerns about the weather, including the tornado warning. He didn't feel the need for any alarm. After all, it was only thunderstorms.

I kept watching. The bad feeling inside of me grew.

I called the dad back, explained how the storm was heading dead east with a tornado warning and I had a really bad feeling. He agreed to ask his boss to leave work early.

The rain and thunder started at 4:55. The boy's dad arrived at five. We chatted for a few minutes. Thirty seconds after his exit, the hail started, approximately 5:05. I ran to the basement to be with my children.

At that time, my boyfriend, Jon, turned on the television in our back bedroom. On the news, the weatherman was talking about a "hook." If it formed, we were in trouble. The next thing I remember is my boyfriend yelling that the hook had formed.

Outside it was black as night. No rain, no wind, no birds.

It was 5:15 when Jon screamed, "Tornado!" He watched it come up over the hill from the Southbridge Airport over Rosemead Apartments.

I pulled my kids over to the chimney. When Jonathan got to the bottom of the basement steps with his grandmother, the tornado was at the edge of our backyard. By the time they reached the chimney area, the tornado was hitting our house—maybe a minute at most had passed.

I've had nightmares about tornados since I was four years old; it's one of my biggest fears. But that day, I knew that if I let fear take over, my children could get harmed, both mentally and physically. I could not let that happen. Somehow, we all stayed calm and spoke quietly.

"Are we going to be okay, Mommy?" Jennifer asked.

"Mommy, what's going on?" Landon wanted to know.

At one point, Jennifer even said, "I will stay strong, and we will be okay."

All I could say was, "We will be okay. I love you. Never forget that. Hold on tight and stay down."

We huddled against the chimney, holding as tight as we could and thinking our lives were over. I kissed both their heads. They started to cry. The tornado sucked the air out of our lungs. That's

when I said, "Grampa, please watch over, shelter and protect us. Dear Lord, take me out if you have to, but leave my children here, unharmed."

If anyone was able protect us now, it would be my grandfather. He passed away when I was ten. As a child, I felt he was the only one who loved, protected and stuck up for me. I was the last one to visit him before he died, aside from my grandmother. And not a day goes by when I don't think of him. I knew he would keep us sheltered and protected.

I will never forget the fear in my body and my children's, or the sensations of it all happening at the same time. The air sucked out of our bodies and it felt like our heads were shrinking and expanding constantly.

And then calm.

Jon, who'd been standing behind me with his hand on my back, backed away, as did his grandmother.

"It's not over! Get back down," I screamed.

I was correct.

Within three seconds, it started up again. This time it pushed open the basement door, right behind us. Cathy ran to shut it and then huddled with us again until the calm returned.

This time, no one moved. We waited.

When it didn't return, we opened the basement door.

Three people ran toward us. "We ran up from Route 169, through the backyard. Is everyone okay?"

"Yes," we replied and sent them on to the next house.

After they left, we saw the disaster.

I made the kids stay in the basement and refused to leave the door. I attempted to call 911 to report the damage, but couldn't get through. Then, I called my father in Woodstock. He's able to see all the way to Southbridge. All he saw were clear skies so he thought my call was a prank. Finally, after nearly three minutes of swearing and my daughter yelling, "It's true! Please believe her!" He did.

Both of my parents jumped in their car as fast as they could. They drove as far as possible.

On the way, he called me. "I'm on the road to your house. Run. Run, now and run fast. Just run and don't stop running!"

I grabbed my children and yelled to their dad. "Let's go! We're running."

At the end of the driveway, a big tree blocked our way.

I panicked and called my dad back. My mom and he had driven as close as they could but were stopped about a mile away by police due to downed power lines and trees.

He calmly said, "Deb, listen to me. Calm down. Just listen and do not panic. You have to run now. Get out of there. Another one is coming."

That was all he needed to say. I picked up my kids and got them over the tree, any way I could, and ran the mile down the road. It was a jumble of a mess. Trees were all over the road and thrown in houses. People were also yelling at us to get home. Another tornado was ten minutes

away. But after what I had already seen, I knew I had to get us out of there. I was looking at something you would see in the movies—except this was real.

When we reached my parents, I realized there were six of us for a five passenger car.

I told my parents to take Jon and the kids: "Leave me here. Just take the kids and keep them safe."

Of course, they refused. We piled four into the backseat and my youngest took my mother's lap in the middle. Yes, it was one hundred percent illegal, but we were six terrified people in a car, seeking safety. At a stop sign, a cop was directing traffic. He winked and waved us on. If I could see him again, I'd shake his hand and thank him. He understood no one was getting out of that end of Charlton Street anytime soon.

We spent that night at my parents' house in Woodstock. For hours, I wondered if we made the right choice. The old wives' tale says that lightning never strikes twice and tornados never follow the same path. Did I put us in more danger by going somewhere the storm hadn't yet hit? Watching the news and the weather did not help. The warnings and watches lasted until around nine o'clock.

My Neighborhood and house!!

Needless to say, we were safe. But still, I wouldn't let anyone out of my sight for the whole evening. The kids had a hard time sleeping unless they were holding me tightly. If I moved or twitched, they were wide-awake. (I didn't sleep again for four days.)

The next day, we all returned home to begin the cleanup of our yard, inside our home and our neighbor's yards. My children didn't seem concerned or afraid, though our house was pretty damaged. The tree that fell in our driveway had shattered one of our windows, turning the glass into dust particles. I had leaves and branches in the house from trees not from my yard.

The shock of the tornado did not fully sink in until a week later, when we moved back into our home. Then, we were afraid all the time, had difficulty sleeping and were constantly thinking about what we had survived. At my parents' house, it felt like a bad dream that hadn't really happened. But once we moved home with the children, we had to face reality.

To this day, if the wind blows, we look to the sky. When it rains, we get scared. And if there's a thunderstorm, we get ready to run to the basement. The kids are afraid to sleep at night. Jennifer has nightmares; Landen won't leave my side.

Without the trees, it's too hot to play outside for long. Both kids beg me daily to move so we will be safe again. It is just no longer home.

Despite all the negatives, we have a great community of support. The Red Cross was amazing, as was the Tornado Relief Group from Spencer. We kept telling everyone we were okay; we didn't need anything. We urged them to help those who'd lost their homes. But the volunteers and workers kept coming, offering us support.

One woman insisted I take water, at least for the kids. I did, even though we had a cooler full. And the next thing I knew, a big empty box hit the tar. She proceeded to empty the contents of her car into the box. "I see it in your face that you're afraid to take from others, but we have so much to give. We want you to have some. Don't worry. We have some for your neighbors, too," she said.

Then, she got in her car and left.

You know, she was one hundred percent right. After our house was ready to live in, I realized I'd thrown out a lot of bedding, clothes, dishes, toys, curtains and so much more than I could afford to replace. It was then I turned to some Facebook pages for help. Springfield Tornado was the first I found, which lead me to the Adopt a Family page. We were adopted by three beautiful families who have forever touched our hearts. We're so thankful and owe so many people a big thank you, starting with Springfield Tornado (New Community Page).

THANK YOU SO MUCH FROM THE BOTTOM OF OUR HEARTS!!!!!!

Denise Vozella
SPRINGFIELD

I was working downtown on the 5th floor of the clock tower building, at the corner of State and Main Streets. Two of us were in that office on June 1st when we saw a debris field in the sky, heading our way. We didn't move right away because we weren't sure what we were seeing. Even when it became clear that it was an actual tornado heading towards us, we still hesitated. I can't explain that.

At some point I became terrified and kicked off my shoes to run down the stairs as fast as I could. I don't mean to be dramatic, but it felt like death was chasing us down those stairs. By the time we made it down five flights to the ground level, there was a woman crouching in the corner of our doorway outside. I went to open it to let her in, but the others inside yelled at me to stop because the tornado was blowing debris through the air. Thank God she ended up being okay.

Before we could even comprehend what was happening, it was over.

After the tornado blew through, I put on my shoes, and took the elevator back to the 5th floor. I was shaking badly, inside and out. My legs felt like jelly. My laptop was still on when I reached my desk, so I posted I had "just been in a friggin tornado!" In retrospect, I'm not pleased with that post. I don't use that language on Facebook and technically, I wasn't in the tornado.

I left the building and walked, in a daze, toward the Civic Center parking garage where my car was parked. I snapped a handful of pictures of Court Square on my cell phone on the way. People were all walking around in a daze. By the time I reached my car, it was less than a half hour after the twister blew through. I turned on the radio station that I used to work for as a newsperson. WHYN's News Director, John Baibak, was apparently on his way to the station but hadn't arrived yet, so they didn't have local programming on. The tornado was being covered at that point by Howie Carr, syndicated on WHYN from Boston. He was taking calls from Springfield. It was the earliest immediate media coverage of the storm, on radio at least.

I had tried calling home on my cell phone, but wasn't able to get through. For some reason, I was able to get through to Howie in Boston. I gave my eyewitness account of seeing the tornado debris field coming towards us from the river, and what was happening downtown in the aftermath. It was strange not being able to go into the radio station, which overlooks Court Square, and cover the story, but hoped my call offered some local perspective to Springfield that day.

It took a long time to get out of the city. The cops kept turning people around at every street I tried to get down because of downed trees, blinking street lights, and chaos. I needed to reach 91 South to get home to Longmeadow. I hadn't been able to reach my daughter on the phone at home, and at that point, didn't know where the storm had headed. Finally, I was able to reach my husband on the phone at his job at Bradley Airport. It was then that I broke down and cried. I was in the car, almost to the highway, and the sky still looked pretty black and scary.

My mother and younger daughter, who had been hunkered down in her school in South Hadley had made it home safely, I learned. My husband got home next, and then I did. That feeling of not being able to be with your loved ones or even get in touch was something none of us will ever forget.

We were glued to the TV coverage all evening and got a lot of calls from friends and family from all over, checking on us here in Western Mass. I ordered Chinese food delivery for dinner and my husband made me a drink. I forget now what it was.

I still don't understand the exact path of the twister took through downtown, but I'm fascinated by how it happened. The tornado went through Court Square, blowing down all those big old trees, and then skipped across to the South End, about a block or two away, devastating all those businesses and homes. Our building was barely touched. How? Maybe it's not something anyone can explain, but I do know I'm thankful it wasn't worse.

Eileen Morin
BRIMFIELD

My sister was working when the tornado hit and could not reach her husband. She called me in a panic to ask for help. My husband and I left our house in Chicopee. We drove to Three Rivers where my sister works and then headed to the campground. We didn't get very far due to the fallen trees in the road and police roadblocks. My sister still did not know the fate of her husband. We called the local hospitals but nothing. By this time we had heard that one person perished at the campground, but we did not know who.

The next day we attempted again to reach to the campground. We pleaded our story to a very nice state police officer who reluctantly let us pass through. It was very difficult getting through due to the debris in the roads. When we reached the campground, well, no words can describe what we saw. Nothing was left. With the help of the National Guard and State Police, a path was constructed using boards and sides of campers that were strewn about, allowing my sister to finally get to her husband.

What a reunion! I never saw my sister cry like that before. My brother-in-law was shaken up and bruised, but otherwise okay. My brother-in-law had been in his camper when the tornado hit. He survived only because the camper broke in half, causing the kitchen cabinets to fall and cover him from all the flying debris. He ended up pinned in the dirt, because there was no floor left. He lay under the camper for an hour until a nearby person heard his screams and rescued him. They then went on to search for other campers. Unfortunately, they found a friend pinned under her refrigerator—the one fatality we'd heard about.

A few other campers made it through, too, and wandered around searching for what might be left of their campers. Everyone was crying and hugging each other. They were devastated because

Village Green Campground is one big family. It was the saddest thing I ever saw, watching people pick up little trinkets they found laying around and trying to salvage anything.

Children's toys, clothes, bedding—you name it—it was everywhere. Some items were actually hanging from the trees. My sister found her beloved birdhouse on the other side of the campground. It was in remarkably good condition.

We left that day with my brother-in-law bruised but thankful to be alive and haunting visions that will stay with us for the rest of our lives.

Erika Torres
SPRINGFIELD

I was working my first job, at a women's health center, when the downpours began on June 1st. I clocked out around 4:00 p.m. to head over to my second job at Modell's. My boyfriend picked me up. On our way, we crossed the Plainfield Bridge. I pointed at this cloud over West Springfield. It looked like it was over Route 5 and resembled a hook in the sky.

About five minutes later, when we arrived to Modell's, that hook of a cloud was right over the parking lot. I kissed my boyfriend and said I would see him later. I told him to text me as soon as he got home. I walked into Modell's, staring in awe at the funny looking shape in the sky. One of my customers was also looking at this cloud. It seemed to be tumbling within itself. I had never seen anything like this before and I've lived my entire life here in Springfield.

I normally go straight to the back and get ready for work. But that day, I couldn't get over this cloud moving quickly over us! So I asked my coworkers if they've noticed how this cloud was acting. No one had even noticed! So, we all walked to the window and stared. It had moved from our parking lot to just behind McDonald's. Keep in mind, only a matter of seconds had passed and there was no noise! No rain, no thunder, no hail, just an eerie silence.

As we watched, I thought that if we stood on top of McDonald's, we would be inside the cloud; it was that low! As it kept tumbling within itself, it kept getting lower and lower. Then, it began to dip and go back up into itself. It kept doing that until it finally began descending slowly. The debris picked up and met the clouds halfway. I was staring at a tornado forming right in front of my eyes—only a couple feet away. I couldn't believe it.

It didn't move for a few seconds. It kept spinning, picking up a ton of debris. At this point, I was shaking and terrified. For those few seconds that it stood, no one knew where it was headed! Then it took off. I panicked when I saw that it turned toward the Memorial Bridge. I called my boyfriend. He said the tornado was in his rearview mirror. Then the call dropped. While my

- 47 -

mind raced, wondering what was going on, I looked outside and saw trees ripped out from their roots. The McDonald's sign landed on top of someone's car. Stop signs were bent like pipe cleaners; houses were missing pieces to their roof; windows on the little shops were blown out. It looked like a ghost town.

The sky turned into the eeriest looking orange. My feet were stuck, I couldn't move from the window. If it weren't for me, some of my customers and co-workers who were just leaving when I arrived, would have been in the middle of everything!

A huge thunderstorm followed. The downpours were so heavy, the roof to Modell's began to leak, and the drain in the parking lot overflowed, turning it into a pond.

Still, to this day, I have nightmares from that.

James Dudley
EAST LONGMEADOW

June 1st was a breezy afternoon. I was at work. I had heard about the tornado warnings and severe thunderstorm warnings/watches from my phone. I was on my way home with my wife when the sky turned really black and gray. Once home, I sat in my kitchen while my mom watched the weather from the broadcast team of WWLP News Team and meteorologists.

One of the meteorologists said, "Go back to that camera; was that a tornado?"

We then saw the powerful swirl on television. It was nerve wracking, scary, and interesting all at once. I sat in the living room, puzzled. My wife and I went out on the porch in East Longmeadow. All of a sudden, the tornado touched down ten feet in front of us. I was scared, so I just sat there. It went away just as fast as it came.

We lost power. When the sky lightened up, we drove around to see all the damage. While in Springfield, there were reports of another tornado coming through. Everyone who was out, scrambled to get back to their houses, cars or any structure that was safer than standing out in the open. My wife, my mom and I were on our way back to East Longmeadow when we hit traffic. The tornado was right behind us. Thankfully, we got home safely.

Around ten o'clock that night, my wife, my dad, brother, mom, and I decided to go to the Red Roof Inn in Enfield, Connecticut. It was pet friendly, so we brought our dog with us. We went home the next day because my parents had gotten a generator from work to power up a fan, the refrigerator and television. We went without power for 60-70 hours.

On the second day, we drove around Springfield again. The damage was devastating, heart wrenching, scary, and just unbelievable. Houses crushed, cars smashed, sidewalks ripped up, trees pulled from their roots, buses/cars and trucks over turned. I just couldn't believe my eyes at everything I was seeing or hearing. The fatalities were low, but still, people died.

The brand new apartments/houses on the side of the Springfield Armory were crushed like a child's toy: one that had been picked up, dropped and then stomped on all over. The damage looked so unreal; it felt to all be a dream. Many roads were closed and there weren't enough police, EMT's, or firefighters to go around, so citizens directed traffic and helped one another. It was heartwarming to see everyone pitching in.

It's going to take a year-and-a-half to rebuild Springfield back to the city it was before June 1st. It will be built better and stronger than ever before. I hope we don't ever go through that again. To this day, the damages are still somewhat bad but getting better. I commend Springfield and all the other towns on their hard work, dedication, and love for where they live and work, also to not let the storm tear our community apart.

Jonathan Hall
BRIMFIELD EMS, PARAMEDIC

On June 1, 2011, I was at home in Brimfield, Massachusetts along with my wife, Amy, who is a Trooper with the Massachusetts State Police. I am a paramedic currently working with several EMS agencies and have been for seventeen years. In total, I've been working in EMS for over 21 years.

At approximately 5:00 p.m., Amy and I heard reports on the local regional radio emergency dispatch out of New Braintree that a tornado was spotted in Springfield. It was headed east, toward Brimfield. My wife and I made some brief efforts to secure our vehicles and property and took shelter in our basement. Shortly after, the tornado passed over, traveling less than 200 feet from our house and continued toward the center of the town.

After the storm passed, we left our house to survey the scene around us. While our home remained intact, our yard was covered with some 20-30 downed trees. We were unable to get our vehicles out of our yard and had lost power and communication. Concurrently, the ambulance and fire pager began to activate, indicating reports of injured persons and building collapses in town. Ensuring that my wife and I were okay, we quickly realized that our assistance was needed for our roles as emergency responders. I grabbed some equipment and walked to the end of our driveway where several cars were stopped due to some downed wires and trees. After helping remove some of the debris blocking the road, I flagged down a person in a passing car who drove me to the ambulance station in the center of town.

There I was assigned by the director of the ambulance service to respond to Haynes Hill Road in town for an individual who was having chest pain. On arrival, we found a woman having cardiac problems in a house that was destroyed by the tornado. We loaded her in the ambulance but were forced to bring her back to the station. All roads in and out of town were blocked by downed trees and debris.

After returning to the station, we began to receive multiple reports of injuries and damage at the Village Green Campground on Route 20. I was dispatched to respond to that scene and was assigned Kate, an EMT with Brimfield Ambulance. We made our way on Route 20 east, toward the campground, attempting to avoid downed wires and debris. Along the two-mile trip, we were slowed several times as we stopped to check on individuals who'd been stranded by the storm because their vehicles or homes had been damaged. We found no severe injuries and advised the individuals to start making their way toward the fire station where a basic triage point was being set up. We also came across a burning vehicle and used a fire extinguisher to ensure that there were no fatalities in the car.

We proceeded onward to the campground. Along the way, we met up with a State Police marked cruiser who assisted us by checking to ensure we would clear trees and wires. At the Campground, we were the first official rescuers to arrive and, along with the State Troopers, began work to assess the scene and provide assistance as needed. We quickly identified that there were two groups involved–those "walking wounded" who were able to approach our staging area and those individuals who were further down in the campground unable to self-extricate themselves and in need of immediate medical care.

Kate and I decided to split up. I stayed at the entrance to the campground establishing an EMS triage. She went to the area with the most destruction. Assisted by several troopers on scenes, Kate performed field assessments and patient extractions.

I think that one of the things that surprised me most was how angry and upset some of the people we first encountered at the campground were. I guess you can't blame them, but it certainly wasn't what I had geared myself up to expect. We were the first sign of help that they saw and we didn't reach the campground until about ninety minutes after the tornado struck. A lot of people told me that things went into a crazy, slow motion pattern for them immediately after the storm. If that was true, then I can only imagine what an hour and a half seemed like waiting for help.

It was a pretty chaotic scene when we first got there—literally people coming out from everywhere. They were bringing up the injured on doors and ladders used as makeshift lifters. I was a little overwhelmed at first. I knew we had limited resources, with only one ambulance.

But what I also knew, but couldn't tell anybody: There was no more help coming for a while.

Based on how long it took us to get to the campground two miles from the center of town and from what I was picking up on the radio, I knew we were going to be on our own, with only the supplies we had on hand.

I think that was the worst part of the day for me.

Thank God I was working with somebody who I knew and trusted. We came up with a quick plan.

"Kate," I said, "take these triage tags and head down to where all the campers are and start figuring out how many people we have here." That was the last I saw of her for awhile. Meanwhile, I stayed up by the ambulance and started taking care of some injured who had already been extricated. With the help of some bystanders, I made a treatment area and tried to figure out about how many people needed care.

This is probably the worst point of any MCI (Mass Casualty Incident) and all the textbooks tell you that if you don't get things right in the first ten minutes, the whole thing can get screwed up.

There were people with a number of different injuries. I remember one young girl with a broken arm and a bunch of people with lacerations and cuts. Then, there were several people with critical injuries. These were the people who were in and near campers during the tornado. Some were in critical condition—maybe four who were pretty messed up with lots of crush injuries and blunt force trauma.

I quickly realized that one ambulance wasn't really equipped to deal with so many patients. All of them got IVs and most received pain medicine. I was just sort of going patient to patient, eyeballing each one, while trying to call for more resources, get things more organized, and make sure that I wasn't missing anything at the same time. I did a few skills in a matter of an hour that I hadn't probably done at all in my prior 17 years of being a medic, including two chest decompressions (needle in the chest to release trapped air) and IOs (a needle access like an IV, but into a bone to give fluids and medications) and lots of pain meds.

I couldn't have done anything that day without the help of a lot of other people who really stepped up to do things that were extraordinary. Civilians at the campground helped us carry and move patients. At some point, a nurse showed up who seemed to know me—I still have no idea who she was—and helped manage some of the sicker patients. I think, overall, we did the best we could with the very limited amount of resources we had.

I stripped about all the gear we had out of the rig—what a mess that was.

Probably, about an hour-and-a-half after we first got there, the first back-up ambulance came to help. By this time, it was getting dark. We had already moved the patients into a half-demolished building when the second tornado passed over. I was beginning to think that some of the patients weren't going to do so well. I remember one guy yelled and cried a lot. And there was another woman, pretty critical, who was really quiet—not talking—just silent, and I knew that wasn't a good sign. She was the first one I decided to send out when the rigs came in.

I will never forget the look on the basic EMT's face when I loaded two critical patients into her ambulance (plus a girl with a fractured arm in the front seat) with IVs and chest needles—sick as hell—and just told her to go—get them to an ER. With fatherly sage advice, I advised, "Just do your best," as I shut the doors on the rig.

I think in total, we saw about 18 patients between the three of us; some with cuts and lacerations, four critical, one DOS (Dead on Scene). Within three hours after we got there, it was over, done; nothing left except to help organize the body recovery of the one who passed away before we even got there.

I was beat. I had worked a 24-hour shift the night before the storm and stayed up all the next day. I went back to the station where, by now, we'd gotten a lot of help from other ambulance services.

I walked into the station, made sure that there were some other ambulances available, and got a ride home.

Sitting in my darkened house, having made my way through a tangle of trees to get home, it was nice to be able to sit in silence for a while.

That was one of the best beers I ever had.

I don't regret anything I did that day. I definitely would've done some things differently, but in retrospect, who wouldn't do something different? If you had to plan your wedding again, you probably would do that differently, or your career, or how you spent your senior year in high school. I often wonder if someone who was more objective than I would have done the same things I did that day. I think it would have been easier if I were a responder from outside the area. Maybe I wouldn't have felt so involved and I could have done a better job.

Most of the time when you go to crazy calls like this, at the end of the shift, you go home and back your normal world. For us in Brimfield, we knew that wouldn't be the case, and that loomed over me.

My house was okay—just a lot of tree work to do—but I knew that wasn't true with the rest of the town. Things had changed and would remain changed for some time.

If you've been in EMS long enough, you are always chasing the dragon. And by that, I mean looking for the big call that's going to make your career. Maybe it's pulling the unconscious baby out of the house fire or the dramatic car wreck that puts you on the front page of the paper. You spend your down time wondering if you'll be up to the task; nobody wants to f* up the big one. I had always gazed at a distant shore in the future looking for my dragon. I never realized I would find him amongst the grass between my barefoot toes in my own backyard. My peers and coworkers have provided words of encouragement and respect for what I did that day, but secretly, I am my own harshest critic.

Jennifer Bouley (Nine years old)
SOUTHBRIDGE

On June 1st 2011, I got off the school bus, had a snack and did my homework. I looked forward to playing outside, as it was a beautiful, hot, sunny day. I got to play outside for about one hour. Then my parents said a bad storm was coming and it was time to get in the house.

My parents were watching the weather and thinking we should go in the basement, "just in case," and play there. So I went around the house and grabbed a few things such as water, my dolls, and all the money I had including Big Y coins. While I was doing this, I noticed it got very dark out. Then it started to hail.

It looked very scary outside. I went into the basement while my mom sat on the steps and my dad watched the weather from the bedroom in the back of the house.

Then my dad screamed, "TORNADO!"

Our lights flickered and then went completely out. My parents grabbed our flashlights as our mom grabbed my brother and me. We ran like crazy through the house, not knowing what to do or where to go or even what was going on.

Finally, we stopped at the chimney and my dad found us there. My brother and I did not know what was going on or if we would be ok. My mother kissed our foreheads and said, "I love you; we will be okay."

When the tornado hit, it felt like the air was just being sucked out of me, I couldn't breathe or anything and my head felt like it was going to EXPLODE. All of a sudden, it went dead calm. My dad was about to open the door and go outside but my mom was screaming, "No, it's not over; stay here; get back; it's only the silent center." Then all of a sudden, the wind and banging started up again.

It stopped about twenty seconds later. We all stayed still to make sure it was actually over. We got up and opened the door only to see the yard was a complete mess and nothing like we left it. We had tree branches in our back yard. A big tree that hit our house covered the driveway, and we had a lot of damage to the back of our house. My mommy tried to call 911 and couldn't get through. She called her dad who did not believe her and she broke down in tears, screaming at him that it was real, not a joke, and it really happened.

I screamed, "Grandpa, please believe her; it really happened!"

My mother would not let my brother and me out of the basement doorway for a long time. She was afraid more would come and wanted us as close to safety as possible. Finally, my grandfather called us back. He said he was here, but couldn't make it down the road. He wanted us to run as fast as we could to get to him and my grandmother. My mother grabbed us and threw us over the tree in our driveway and we ran like the wind.

People were yelling at us to "go back home, get inside, another is coming."

My mother refused to listen and we just ran. We found my grandma and grandpa. My mom, my dad, my brother, my grandma, and grandpa piled in the car and we went to their home in Woodstock for a week.

My thoughts before the tornado was: why was everyone acting all crazy? I kept wondering what was going on. It was chaos. I got all confused, I didn't know what to do. I did my best to stay calm and do everything my mom said. My stomach started to feel icky and I got very worried and nervous.

My thoughts and feelings during the tornado: I thought we were not going to make it. All my stuff would be gone. I wouldn't have my bed or my pictures. I was afraid something bad would happen to my brother or parents. I didn't know if I would live!!

My thoughts right after the tornado: I wondered if my friend a few houses down was okay. I wondered if it (the tornado) was coming back. I also wondered what the front of our house looked like. I was very scared. Everything became real. I was in complete shock.

The night of the tornado: I was sleeping at my grandparents. It took me a long time to get to sleep and I could not leave my mom's side. I had a very bad dream that I still have every night. I was very scared to go to sleep. I didn't want to. I also could not eat.

The following week: we came home two days after the tornado and helped clean up the yard and neighbor's yard. I was thinking I was glad everything and everyone was as good as it could be. I still had a really bad icky feeling. I didn't wanna be here. I did not want to come back home.

As time went on, I started to feel better and less worried. I felt only a little bit safer. I know and understand life will never be the same and I will never take it the same again. I think more about life, weather, and family in a more caring way. I realize just because I am here today doesn't mean I'll be here tomorrow. I also learned not to be so needy and greedy. I should be happy for what I have and accept what I can get, rather than want more, because other children lost everything they owned and I still have a lot of my things. I also learned that there are not only bad people in this world, like the news makes it out to be. We have wonderful people in this world who are caring and giving even for strangers.

We are grateful for the families who adopted us and helped give us some clothes and toys from near and far away who have never met or knew us before.

I typed this up for Jennifer; she really wanted to do it. I told her I didn't know if it would make the book, but maybe it would help her re-live it and get it off her chest. I also told her you would like to read her story. I typed as she spoke and tried to make the best full sentences as I could.

Big Y coins... a local grocery store gives you coins to use at your next visit to get a discount on gas at the local gas station or money off a certain food on sale in the store. I laugh now that she packed it, but when I first saw them I was like.. what the heck... and her thought at the time was if we needed to go food shopping and we didn't have any money except hers, we could get food cheap with all the coins she had. Hehehehe so cute... gotta love her!

Thanks for letting her do this and thanks for taking the time to read her story.

I asked my son; he didn't want any part of reliving the tornado. He is still a mess at times when he thinks of that day.

— Debra Bouley

Kimberly Lauren
SPRINGFIELD

Well, June 1st was just like any other day. I left work around two o'clock with my three-year-old son (I work at his school). My seven-month-old son, who attends the same school but at a different center, would be dropped off at home via school bus at 4:30 p.m., as usual. Then, I planned to go to the laundromat with my neighbor.

It was extremely hot that day. I'd been texting a friend of mine when I became aware of a tornado warning. I turned my TV on to the news, where they had the camera focused on some clouds. As they were speaking about the changes in clouds that indicate warning, the TV cut out! At the same time, my youngest son's school bus beeped the horn downstairs. I instructed my three-year-old to stay inside while I ran out to the bus.

The driver warned me to be careful—the clouds were spinning and the funnel was right behind the house next to my building on Central St. I grabbed my son and ran like I never have up three flights of stairs! My heart pounded. I have never seen anything like what I witnessed: the funnel cloud was incredibly close. I saw bricks and boards and debris spinning through the air. It was like something straight out of a movie.

As I got back into my house, I planted my three-year-old and his brother in the closet. I lay over them, praying to God to keep my babies safe. The sounds we heard as we huddled together without seeing anything were incredible: glass shattering and structures crumbling. The whistling of the wind was beyond words.

When all seemed quiet, I slowly exited the closet. I told my kids to stay put while I looked around. Tree branches, mud and glass were everywhere. The bathroom ceiling had caved in. All the windows were shattered and the frames had been blown in. I opened my front door. There should have been a porch, but the porches were collapsed. I was devastated to see my family's home in this condition.

I panicked and grabbed some shoes for my son, a can of formula for my baby, and my phone charger. I headed through the living room to move branches off the couch to attempt exit through the hallway and make it the three stories down.

The awning over the door had fallen. A large tree had uprooted from across the street and lay in the alleyway between the two buildings. My children and I climbed over and under fences to get away from the building. The streets were flooded with police. Residents aimlessly walked around. I just continued thanking God that my children were unharmed.

We were helped to walk down to Main Street.

My three-year-old began violently vomiting due to his nerves.

We eventually made it to the Mass Mutual Center and began trying to contact family and friends.

Our home was looted that night, but one month to the day after the tornado, my family was blessed with a new home. Unfortunately, my three-year-old has had adjustment issues. He's been in therapy to try and help him overcome fears and bring some kind of closure regarding the tragedy in his young life.

June 1st and the experience that followed, was a day I will never forget. I pray all the affected families are helped in getting their lives back on track. I hope my family's story can help.

Lauren Ladue
SPRINGFIELD

On June 1st, 2011, my home was destroyed by the tornado. My grandmother, my sister-in-law, my six-month-old nephew, and I were in my house at the time. It was just another day to me. I was enjoying the light thunderstorm as it was coming in. I walked outside and tried to save a caterpillar cocoon from the storm, while mumbling, "I'd better get some good karma for this." What I received was quite the opposite.

I came inside and watched the storm from my window. Then, I noticed the abnormality of the wind. I saw branches about the size of my arm flying, and the heavy lawn chairs weightlessly get tossed across my front lawn. I knew this was serious. I grabbed my phone and ran for my door, only to see Caitlyn, my-sister-in-law, holding my nephew. She wanted to come in my room because the storm was scaring the baby. As we talked about it, my windows smashed from the wind. Caitlyn told me to wake up my grandmother and get her in the basement.

Panicking, I told my grandmother we had to get in the basement. She, being a strong woman, questioned why we needed to go. Finally, after I yelled, "Grandma, there's a tornado; we have to go!" She got up.

Caitlyn told me to take my nephew and hide under the stairs in the basement. I only remember getting to the top of the stairwell. I was already breathing in debris from the tornado, and it hadn't even reached full force yet. After that, I blacked out. I remember huddling under the stairs in the basement, covering every inch of my nephew's body with my own, in a fetal position. Caitlyn was upstairs helping my grandmother down into the basement. They got past my bedroom just in time to see the beam collapse and everything cave in.

Once we were sure the tornado had passed, Caitlyn went first up the stairs to find an exit.

Since there was woods right next to our house, the entire forest looked as if someone had taken a chainsaw and cut all the tops of the trees off and dumped them on my street. My bedroom had a door leading outside, yet my room was demolished. The only other door led to the driveway, which was covered in trees. We had to exit through a window. I managed to find shoes to put on in the only untouched room, and I hopped out the window. Unknowingly, I sliced my leg open during the jump. With my adrenaline pumping, I wasn't aware until my neighbor pointed it out.

I took my nephew out and left him with a neighbor while I carried Caitlyn out. My grandmother didn't trust Caitlyn and me to help her out the window, so she was trapped for a bit. Caitlyn, who is CPR certified, left to check on the neighbors. In the process of doing so, she luckily came across two men who were delivering a refrigerator at the time of the tornado. She asked them to help my grandmother out of the window. Finally, she was able to get out.

After that, we went into our neighbor's basement in case another tornado was to occur. After twenty minutes of calling friends and family to make sure they were okay, we decided to go back outside. At that point, my brother, Ian, had left work and managed to climb over live wires and under trucks to make sure we were all safe. A little after that, my sister Hillary arrived on the scene. Ian and Hilary tried to obtain some valuables from the house before fleeing.

Around that time, the firemen arrived and were helping the elderly in the neighborhood. One of the firemen had been told that another tornado was going to touch down in fifteen minutes. Everyone started running towards the next street over to make it to the main street, Island Pond Road. Once we got there, we saw many people wandering with nothing but their kids and people escaping in their cars. It was pouring, and the sky was a bright yellow-orange. We came across an old family friend's house and hid out there until my boyfriend's father could pick us all up.

During that time, I was enduring an extreme panic attack, barely able to breathe. Once our ride came, we all packed in and a newsman came up to our car. He asked us a bunch of questions until my sister Hillary insisted he leave us alone. From there, we drove through quite a bit of flooding and ended up stopping at a convenience store in Chicopee. The man working was nice enough to give us discounts on things such as diapers and formula, as well as some food.

Once everyone was able to relax, we were overjoyed that we all had made it out alive. We drove to Caitlyn's mother's house, where Caitlyn, Ian, my nephew and I started our lives over from scratch. My grandmother ended up living with my uncle. That moment in time has forever changed us, and I know we all appreciate life a little more after that day.

Monica Donnelly
WEST SPRINGFIELD

I live on Irving Street in West Springfield. I was nine months pregnant with our second child, scheduled to give birth via C-section on June 7th. So, June 1st was my last day of work before maternity leave. I wanted to take a few days off before Jayson arrived so that I could get stuff in order.

It's a gorgeous day out, June 1, 2011. And, to top it all off, it's my husband's birthday. We plan to go to his favorite place to eat.

At 2:00 p.m., my phone rings.

It's a friend calling. "Hey dude, there's a tornado warning for the area. So I just want to let you know. Stay safe!"

I respond with, "What? Are you kidding?"

He assures me he's not. I log onto the local news channel. Sure enough, TORNADO WATCH is written right across the website. I waddle into my manager's office to tell her the news.

She's in shock, too, but says the same thing we're all thinking, "We can't get a tornado here."

It's now 3:00 p.m. The news site says: TORNADO WARNING.

My manager sends an email, notifying everyone of the warning and what precautions to take. I am on the Safety Committee and a Floor Warden at work, serving as a certified first responder. It's my responsibility to help lead everyone to safety in the event of an emergency. I laugh about it all the time because I get to wear a cool orange vest and be the last out of the building. It's fun and comical on drill days. Not so much today.

My co-worker, who used to live in Oklahoma, tells us, "A tornado can't happen here" and it's just "going to be a really bad storm." He describes what happens during a tornado. We're all fascinated. Some of us laugh it off. Others get scared. I'm not really scared; it's my last day of work. I can't wait to get home. I also think how it would be a drag if we couldn't go to dinner and I have to cook.

I call my husband, Jay. "Babe, there is a tornado watch."

He responds, "Really? Cool!" We chat about tonight and how if it is raining too hard, we won't go to dinner. He also suggests he pick up Riley from the babysitter. Then, check the weather when he gets home.

It's 3:45 p.m. Jay calls. The radar on The Weather Channel shows the storm is in the Northampton/ Holyoke area. It doesn't appear anything will hit us in Springfield. I tell him how great that is (now I may not have to make dinner after all) and then remind him I may be home a little late because I have a few things to finish since it's my last day.

It's 4:07 p.m. My supervisor and I chat about last minute stuff. My phone rings.

It's Jay. "Get in your car and come home NOW!" He says that the storm shifted on the radar and is headed right for us. He tells me that they are reporting hail in Northampton. He doesn't want me to drive in this.

After I tell him I can't leave, he argues with me.

Finally, my supervisor and I agree that I should go and come back tomorrow to button things up.

I leave.

It is 4:20 p.m. I arrive home. Jay, my sister, her friend, and my mother are on the porch. It has started to rain. Clouds are forming, so we know a thunderstorm is coming. I tell them about what my co-worker said about tornados in the area. And what happens when one forms. "He said that everything stops. Not gradually, like immediately. The rain, the wind. He said it gets kind of eerie out…"

My sister, Jen, takes pictures of the clouds above my neighbor's house. Jay seems to not be paying attention to me.

Suddenly, Jay yells, "Go get in the basement… now."

I scoop up our three-year-old daughter, Riley, and head for the basement. Jen is in front of me. We hit the top of the stairs and the power goes out. We hear the sound of wind, but it sounds a thousand times louder than any I've ever heard.

I hear my mom demanding that I give her Riley. I don't have time to think about that. It's so dark. We are fumbling down the stairs. Finally, we make it to the basement. I tell everyone to just stand in the middle. And now I wait for Jay. He's not coming. I'm nervous. I hope he was just being dramatic, even though that's not like him.

He follows shortly after.

He tells us he saw the tornado touch down in a parking lot. I notice daylight outside again. When we first got down here, it looked dark as night out those windows. Jay yells that he sees our neighbor outside. I tell him to go get her, because in my mind, the tornado is still happening outside. She is unsafe.

Jay yells down to the basement. It's safe. We can come up.

I walk outside slowly, not sure what I am going to see. The big tree in front of the house across the street has been uprooted. It has landed between two houses, resting its branches on the roofs and porches of each house.

I hear sirens in the distance. There are so many people on our street. I don't recognize half of them. Where did they come from? Who are they? I thank God it's just one tree that is damaged in our yard. I don't even think about the rest of the neighborhood. I hear birds chirping. I hear more sirens.

Mom tries to call Dad. Her phone won't connect. I try it on my phone. It works. "Dad? Are you ok? Where are you?" I can tell he's driving from the background noise.

He gives back the answer I knew he would. "Driving home from work. Why?"

I tell him a tornado just touched down in our neighborhood. I tell him about the destruction all around us. "Dad, there's a guy stuck in a car on Main Street. You can't get into our neighborhood from either end."

He's in shock. He can't grasp what I am saying. And he has no idea what he is in for when he drives up to our neighborhood.

Next I call my older sister. She is in the basement of her office building. They saw the tornado out the window over the river and evacuated immediately.

That reminds me: my co-workers. I call Jill. She answers. She's not at work, though. She left early to go to Dakin Animal Shelter to pick up a foster cat. She tells me she is okay. She was in the shelter when it happened. Her car, however, is not okay.

My text messages start coming through faster than I can respond. "The news just mentioned your street. Is it true? A tornado?" and "OMG are you ok?" I can tell some of my friends are frantic.

Panic sets in now. This is real, this really happened.

Jay and my sister go off to explore the neighborhood and see the damage. He wants to check on his shop to see if there is any damage there. Maria, my sister's friend, grabs her camera. I can't go because I have Riley. We don't know what's out there; I don't want to push it.

They come back with an unimaginable report. Cars are crumpled and have been thrown around. Tractor trailers overturned. Buildings missing their top floors. Houses crumbled. Houses shifted off of their foundation. Just about every tree: GONE. The other streets are barely passable on foot. You cannot drive down them. People are wandering around in a fog, not knowing what to do.

My immediate reaction is to help. I want to walk through the neighborhood and offer assistance, but I can't. I'm pregnant.

So many people are on our street. They have come to see the tornado aftermath, first hand. There are cars parked up and down each side. People take pictures. Ask questions. The ambulances can't get down the street. One ambulance worker has to get out and move a bystander's car just to get by. We are angry. We yell at these people to get out of here. Not because we don't think they should see, but because we know there are people hurt or worse and they can't get the help they need. Not to mention, Dad still isn't home. He's stuck in traffic because people are flooding our neighborhood to gawk.

Jay's mom calls. His grandparents in Sturbridge were hit by the tornado, too. His grandmother can't get home and his grandfather is stuck in the house with no electricity. There are so many trees down in their neighborhood so there isn't one clear road. I can see the look in Jay's eyes. He is worried. I tell him to go try and get to his grandparents. We are safe here. But he doesn't want to leave. He is worried I will go into labor. He is worried Riley and I will need him. Part of me is glad he wouldn't go. The other part of me is sad we can't go and help them.

About an hour passes; then, we get word that another storm burst may be hitting. We rush down to the basement with the kids and some neighbors. We give the kids PB&J and juice boxes and wait.

Riley says, "Mama, why do we have to be in the basement? I am not allowed to come down here."

What do I say? How do I answer? "Riley, we have to stay down here for just a little bit until it is safe."

It is raining now, pretty hard. We can still see rescue workers driving through. Each one stops and asks if we are safe. Around 7:00 p.m., the power goes out. We are informed we won't have electricity for a while because they need to shut it off in order to start fixing the power lines. Around 7:30, my husband, sister, and neighbor decide to try to go to a store to get drinks and snacks for everyone. All the neighbors are just sitting on each other's porches, still in awe of what happened.

I get a text message from a friend, she's in another, unaffected part of town and has power. She also informs me that the news reports another tornado heading for us. They even gave a time on the news: 8:12 p.m. It is 7:50.

I call Jay, "Where are you?" He tells me the officials have blocked off our area and won't let him come home.

Now, I panic.

I start crying.

I need to get Riley to the basement; I'm exhausted, emotional, and just cannot stand the thought of something happening and Jay not being here with us.

"Mama," Riley says, "don't cry, I'm right here. It's okay."

Great, I think, my three-year-old is comforting me! We head to the basement, for the third time. Jay finally convinces a police officer that he needs to get to me because I am pregnant and due any day now. By the time he returns, it's deemed safe again by the news. We emerge from the basement.

The electric company says we won't have power for a few weeks.

I start to panic again.

A few weeks? What? How am I going to bring home a new baby, to a house with no electricity?

The National Guard comes around the neighborhood. They have big trucks and guns! GUNS?! They ask if everyone is ok and how many people live in the house. They have orange spray paint cans and spray paint an "X" on houses and sidewalks. I ask the man what that is for. He tells me it is how they count how many people are injured, alive, dead, and staying in the houses or leaving.

We are told we cannot be out after dark and once we leave, we cannot come back.

Now, I officially lose it. I just start crying hysterically.

HOW CAN THIS BE HAPPENING?

HOW? HOW? HOW?

I decide I can't be here. I have to leave. I start packing. We head for my sister's. I tuck Riley into bed and fall asleep in her living room chair. I wake up around 1:00 a.m. with serious contractions. They are four minutes apart and very strong. I try to stay calm. This baby cannot come out yet. He needs to stay in there until things at home are normal. Fortunately, they aren't progressive labor.

We awake the next morning pretty early. Jay and I decide to leave Riley with my sister. We head home to see what we can gather and figure out what is the next step for our neighborhood. As we try to enter, a police officer stops us. He won't let us through by car. He tells us we can walk. Jay points to my belly. That doesn't convince the officer. He still says no.

Jay parks in a parking lot and starts to walk. I stay in the car and cry again. Finally Jay calls. If I go to Main Street, that officer will let me in.

We get home. And still have no power. Some people say one more day, others say weeks. I pack up as much as I can. If I leave, I may not get back in. Jay decides he is going to stay at the house. He and my dad are going to get a generator to keep an eye on things.

My phone rings. It's my manager. She tells me all my co-workers are safe and asks if I need anything.

I spend the next two days camped out at my sister's house, freaking out about all the stuff I need to get done. I pray so hard for electricity again in our house and on Friday, power is restored. We are able to return home. We are so thankful!

Friday evening, I ask Jay to drive me through the neighborhood so I can see the area. We get halfway, and I just can't take it. How could I be complaining about electricity when all of these people lost their homes? In some of those houses, people were injured, or worse.

I feel sadness, anger, anxiety. The neighborhood feels bare. It is unrecognizable. In that moment, I realize the magnitude of the tornado on the entire community. And, I realize how lucky I am that it completely missed our house and my family was unharmed.

When we drive through the neighborhood today, Riley still asks questions. Recently, she said in a car ride, "Daddy, why did the tornado tear down those houses?"

He responded with, "Because it was really strong wind, Riley, and that's what tornados do."

"But Daddy, why didn't the tornado tear down our house," she asked.

I held my breath as he answered, "Because, Riley, someone really, really, really loves you."

"No, Daddy, it's because God saved us," she said.

Scott Kier

EMS SUPERVISOR/PARAMEDIC, SPRINGFIELD MA

June 1st started out as a typical day for me. On my "two days-two nights" schedule of work. I spend most of that last day in bed sleeping. This day was no exception. My shift on the night of May 31st wasn't very memorable or busy; still, overnights can get long and sleep was on the menu for me.

I awoke that day sometime around 1:00 p.m. My plan was to go to a local book store, have a cup of coffee and write a bit before I headed back to work that night. I showered and my uniform was ready to go by about 2:00 p.m. Anyone who knows me will tell you that this very unusual. Normally, I'm scrambling to get ready for work at the last minute and head out the door for my short commute to the station. But this day was different. I was ready to go long before my shift. Although I had tentative plans, I cannot help but think that there was something else at work that day.

My neighbor knocked on my door about an hour before everything hit. He's a nice guy, a great neighbor and is well aware of how grueling my schedule can be. "Hey, I figured you were sleeping and I wanted to make sure you knew we had a tornado warning today."

I shrugged it off, like all the other tornado warnings I'd seen in my fourteen years in Massachusetts. I was of the same thinking as many of my friends and peers: "It'll never happen here."

After looking at the weather radar for the western part of the state, I decided to skip the bookstore and hunker down for what looked to be a pretty spectacular storm headed our way. The power that Mother Nature possesses has always fascinated me. I've both lived and worked through my share of snowstorms, hurricanes, storms, and heat waves in my town and they've always presented their own unique challenges. I wondered if this one would prove to be similar. I put my feet up on my desk, turned my scanner on and went back to doing the work I'd initially slated for the bookstore.

That is when the hail started. It seemed to come out of nowhere. It didn't last very long, but it definitely caught my attention. I had not seen hail in a long, long time. In fact, I couldn't tell you the last time I saw it. I took another glance at the radar and could already tell that things were getting worse. By my assumptions, this bad thunderstorm would have passed by the time I was ready to go to work.

When the tornado touched down near the Memorial Bridge, the Springfield Police Department was right there with a front row seat. I thought, *This will be interesting. It will probably stay on the Connecticut River and we will have a great story to tell about the near miss we had.* That's when it turned toward the city and started tearing its path of destruction. I sat, listening to the police officers in downtown Springfield calling out the tornado's path like a car chase; then, listening to their reports of the damage left in its wake. I knew, then, it was time to head into work. I couldn't see any point in waiting for a call that everyone was too busy to make.

As I listened, I dismissed the complete unpredictability of tornados. Instead, I started frantically getting myself ready for work, much like what I would have at 6:00 p.m. on any normal night, and headed in when the tornado was somewhere near the middle of the city. Days after, I had people telling me how they retreated to their basements or got themselves to what they felt was the safest spot in their house. Ironically, the thought of doing that never crossed my mind. All I could think about was getting to work, hitting the streets.

On my way in, I called my parents, both EMTs, in New Jersey. I always promised them I'd keep them updated if anything "big" ever happened and this was the biggest thing I'd encountered. My message was short: "Hi, it's me. Call me."

After arriving at work, I found myself a partner. We headed toward downtown Springfield in our ambulance. I was anxious and excited, not knowing what to expect when I got there. When we train for mass casualty incidents, we are usually shown pictures of a variety of gruesomeness. We're taught to expect the worst: dead bodies, severely injured people, and a slew of potential hazards that could make our job harder. All of this rushed through my mind as I prepared for what we might see. The ride down State Street probably took about six minutes, but it felt like the longest ride ever. I sat in the passenger seat of our truck, listening to the radio traffic with my brain running through every conceivable scenario it could come up with.

I had already heard one of our ambulances had set up a "casualty collection point" on one of the downtown streets, so that became our destination.

We arrived on Main Street just south of State Street to find a sea of people walking north out of the south end toward what they felt was the most logical shelter: the Mass Mutual Center. My crews were staged near the south end community center, finishing up their operations there. The most vivid memory I have was the strong, almost overwhelming smell of natural gas filling the air. It was so bad that it did not take long for me to develop a headache. I didn't know how bad of a gas leak we were dealing with, but at that point, I didn't really think it mattered. It was not going to change anything that was going on.

Crews had already collected a few patients and were loading them for transportation to one of the area's hospitals. We determined that there was nothing more to do, so we decided to move south through the crowd with our trucks. There were a few ambulances only a couple of blocks away, but we had not made contact with them via the radio or otherwise. We moved south on Main Street collecting other ambulances as we went. Miraculously, our patient count was extremely low. Somehow, not many people had been injured. Hearing that other areas were potentially worse and other crews needed more help, we started moving some of the ambulances out of the area and toward the center of the city.

By the time we got to the Dunkin Donuts in the South End of Springfield, rumors that another tornado had touched down were flying around. Luckily for us, this was also the location where many of the news outlets had setup. I grabbed one of the reporters from a Connecticut station and had him get us a weather report from his studio. The picture they had was not clear either, so we made the decision to move even farther south. From there, we had a better vantage point and an easier time moving if necessary.

We settled into a large parking lot south of where we had been. By this time, there were five ambulances with us. That was when I finally felt my phone ringing. It was my mother, still completely unaware of what we were facing.

"I just want you guys to know I am okay," I said.

My mother asked, "What happened?"

"A tornado just went through Springfield. It's bad."

She wished me well and spent the next four hours with a close friend, a bottle of wine, and the Weather Channel, doing her best to keep track of me.

Once it seemed like the danger passed, we moved back north. Making our way slowly up to State Street and Main Street, we touched base with some Springfield Police Officers who reported they were considering the area all clear. It was time to move off to other areas. There was more work to be done.

After we left downtown, the group of ambulances we collected headed off to Island Pond Road, arguably the hardest hit area of the city. Springfield was effectively "cut in half" by the tornado, and we were on the northern edge of the southern part of the city. Island Pond Road is a well-traveled main artery running north to south through the city. Although I could talk to my crews only a quarter-mile to the north, I could not see or get to them.

During our time on Island Pond Road, we were all on "high alert." The sky turned a shade of green I'd never seen before. The fears of another tornado coming grew. A large number of people from the community had come to seek help and shelter, so none of us (medics/EMTs) spoke of the potential dangers we were facing. We all knew the risks, though.

Prior to our arrival, the fire department and one of our ambulance crews had taken over a small convenience store to use as temporary shelter. There was nowhere else for us to go at that point. If another tornado came through, things could have gotten ugly rather quickly. Thankfully, it didn't. The fire captain who was on scene got us some bottled water and snacks from the owner, which helped us all recharge.

For the next couple of hours, the number of people with us increased. Two of our crews had spent a half hour in a Good Samaritan's basement with about twenty-five other people until it was safe enough to move them to a temporary shelter just north of us. Gradually many of the people who remained with us found their own rides from family members and friends. Eventually the decision was made to move all the ambulances in the city to the Basketball Hall of Fame. This became our unofficial home for the next three or four days.

Arriving there was like a big reunion. Everyone reunited with voices they'd heard on the radio. We celebrated that everyone was safe and unhurt. We also joked, hugged and bonded, dealing with the stress of June 1st in a way that only seventy or eighty EMTs and paramedics could.

In the days that followed, we ran an EMS operation like one I'd never seen. Everyone was willing to work long hours. Everyone wanted to be there. Everyone wanted to contribute what they could. We were closely tied to the Massachusetts State Police. They took good care of us. Also, the generosity of the businesses in the city was something to behold. Every night a different restaurant showed up with an amazing spread of food or coffee. Cell phone companies offered free Wi-Fi to all the emergency workers. The teamwork of the city was amazing.

Gradually, things got back to normal. Within a week, our crews were back on their usual street corners responding to emergencies just like they would have on May 31st. Streets were cleared, and before long, it was business as usual for us.

The truth of it all is: I didn't do very much that day. I never laid a hand on a patient or even put on a pair of gloves. I didn't pull anyone out of a house or perform any "life-saving" interventions. Those around me were the true heroes: the police officers, the firefighters, and my often overlooked and forgotten colleagues in EMS who were going door to door collecting frightened and lost people.

When it was all said and done, I reflected back on that day and realized how difficult communicating with my friends and family was. Cell phone service was spotty. Text messages went through, occasionally. We all had people out there who worried about us. For me, it was my parents and someone I had become close to who was hunkered down with her son, unsure what to expect next. I kept in touch as best as I could, but as one would imagine, we were busy that day. When the time came to speak to those we cared about, everything going on around us seemed to slip into slow motion. Nothing was more important in those moments than letting them know we were safe.

Sometimes, I feel like I was more of a witness than a participant in everything that happened. Then someone reminds me that even though I wasn't up front and elbow deep in the action, the role I played was pretty important.

As for those who were closer to the "front lines," I could not have been more proud of them. They put their own well-being and safety aside, selflessly, for the benefit of others. Whether any of us admitted it or not, we were in harm's way that day, but that did not matter. Taking care of the people that we encountered was all that was on our minds.

On more than one occasion, I have had people I work with or know from the industry say to me, "Hey, I heard you did a pretty great job on the day of the tornado."

I just smile and thank them, and that is usually when the story swapping commences. Because everyone has a story from that day, whether they were there or not.

I heard the tornado warnings on the radio while I was at work. Like most people, I really didn't take them seriously. I tried to leave work on time at 4:00 but was unable to finish up until 4:30. As I walked to my car, I noticed that the sky was brown. It was extremely windy. I walked past a man sitting in his truck and said to him, "This should be interesting."

He agreed and I was on my way.

I live a couple miles from work. I take East Alvord Street from Sumner Avenue to Island Pond Road. As I was driving on East Alvord, I saw small branches in the street and trash cans knocked over. People were walking out of their houses, looking at the sky. I thought, *Relax people; it's only wind!*

When I got to Island Pond Road, though, things started to look a little different. The tree at the corner was blown over. A telephone pole in front of Rocky's Ace Hardware leaned toward the street. I assumed the wind did this. But the further I drove down Island Pond Road, the more my jaw dropped. The sign at Murphy's convenience store was gone. I saw more and more trees down. One tree had fallen across Island Pond between Agnes and Rosella Streets. I live on Rosella and couldn't get through. I decided to turn onto Agnes since it connects to Rosella from Arcadia.

On Agnes Street, I finally saw the devastation. Trees and power lines

covered the street. There was no way through. I turned around and parked my car at the Advance Auto Parts store and walked. I got to the end of my street when I received a text from my mother that read, "Tornado hit your house. Where are you?" The day before she had arrived from Buffalo, New York to visit; she was at the house when the tornado hit.

I replied that I was at the end of the street and asked if she was okay. She said she was. I made my way to the house. I can usually see my house from

the corner of Island Pond and Rosella but because of all the trees down, I couldn't see past the second house. I climbed over the debris and got to my house just as my mother came out. A tree lay across my roof. There was a 4x6 foot section of roofing on my lawn and a 2x4 through my mother's car window. Trees and power lines were down. It was hard to imagine what happened.

I went into the front of my house, then out the back door to check on the

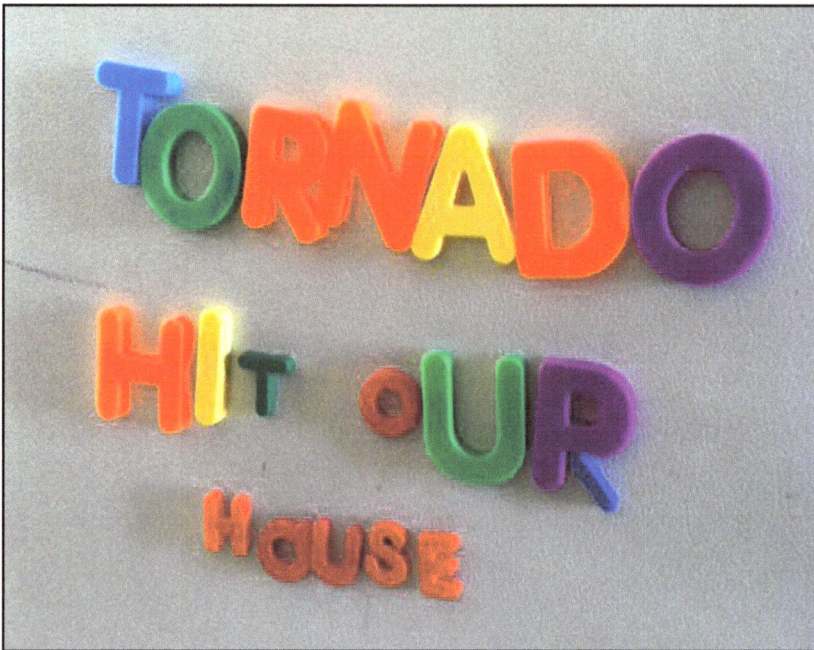

damage. The neighbor's tree landed on my house, but from what I could see, it did very little damage. Three trees in my back yard fell on my daughter's swing set. I found another 4x6 sheet of plywood with shingles in my back yard. I don't know where either of them came from. My roof was still relatively intact.

After looking around the neighborhood, I guessed my house caught the edge of the tornado. My mother was able to get to the basement in time, only because she was watching television and they broke into her program. She saw video of the tornado coming across the Connecticut River. All I can think about was how I could have been caught in the worst of it—if I'd gotten out of work on time. If I left work even five minutes earlier, I probably would have been in my driveway at the moment it hit.

Stacey Dill
MONSON, MA

Atypical June afternoon ended up being a day that changed our lives. Matthew, my husband, was home on vacation. He kept busy preparing our house for the sale we dreamt would take us somewhere with a larger yard and closer proximity to work. My three children and I gathered at home after school, as we normally did. My oldest, fourteen-year-old Haley, busied herself on the phone in her upstairs bedroom. Ally, thirteen, and Russell, nine, requested to walk the short

trip on Main St to the library. I instructed them to stay together until I picked them up at 5:00 p.m. They agreed.

But at approximately 4:15 p.m, Ally and Russell walked in the door, thankfully together. Still, I gave them the hairy eyeball for deviating from the plan. It's important I know where everyone is at all times, even though we live in a cozy, "Main Street, USA" type of town. Ally told me to relax, grabbed her overdue book, and said they could walk back to the library, no harm done. I opened the door with a huff and noted the weather. Feeling totally justified, I snapped, "Now it's raining, and you're not going anywhere." They hung their heads in defeat.

I checked Facebook, as I often do throughout the day. A friend posted an update that her son was

scared of a tornado warning on the news. I didn't give it a second thought. Born and raised in East Longmeadow, I was very accustomed to the "Emergency Response Network" television interruptions. Surely, this was another false alarm.

Even a little later, when Ally and Russ discovered hail shooting down from the sky, we played carefree on the porch. But, baseball-sized hail leaves baseball-sized welts, so I told the kids to come inside. I still had no idea what was coming when I sat on the couch next to my husband. We didn't have a basement, so I asked, "Where would we go if there really was a tornado?" It was only a question.

And then my children ran toward us, pale and frightened. They saw parts of houses, trees and even a squirrel whipping through the air. The clouds were dark and moving extremely fast.

"Get in the laundry room!" I shouted, just as tree branches crashed through our living room window, accompanied by the sound of breaking glass. We ran to the laundry room, the children in front and the adults bringing up the rear. I felt the glass chasing at my heels, grazing the back of my leg.

Head count: two kids.

There should be THREE.

God knows what pummeled the house, but I HAD TO FIND HALEY.

I ran to bottom of the stairs and pulled on the living room door. The suction held it closed. Summoning all my strength, I pulled again, and it opened. I think I was screaming her name. But either way, she called out from under a clothes rack, right on the other side of that door. I led her by the hand into the laundry room.

Matthew ran upstairs to evaluate the situation, but could only describe it as "not good." I started to seriously question our safety. Still, because Haley feared losing her dance

trophies and pictures, I ran back to her room to retrieve them. It was then I heard the loud familiar rumble of a freight train screaming by and saw our roof come inside the house—right into her room.

I returned to my family and deposited Haley's treasures in the dryer. Through the chaos, I saw my son clutching his stuffed doggy tight. "Are we going to be ok?" he asked.

"Yes, of course, just hold on." I told him, but only because I knew it was the right thing to say. Honestly, I had no clue what the hell was going on; or if, in fact, we were going to be ok.

I made two more mad dashes out of that laundry room while the storm raged. First, to get my dog, who was hiding under the shed and then to open the bathroom window, trying to minimize damage. Upon opening that window, I felt the strongest and most unusual suction. Just like a huge vacuum pulling on me from outside. I was scared. The only way I can describe how I felt is to compare it to another time I had experienced fear like this: the day my father died. It was as if my insides turned completely liquid and released themselves. (Yes, I wet myself.)

After maybe twenty minutes, the atmosphere seemed to calm. I told my family to stay in the laundry room while I explored. The living

room was covered in glass, some of it embedded in deep gashes in the walls. Tree branches lay everywhere. Both the rear door and second story doors were badly damaged and partially blocked by a tree. Through the front door, I saw our electric meter draped over my minivan in the driveway. Finally, I decided to exit through the rear sliding door. I was forced to climb over a fallen tree and chain link fence.

Once outside, I saw leaning electric poles, crushed cars, a woman covered head to toe in soot, twisted metal and toppled trees. There was even some melted asphalt that bubbled up like thick pea soup, probably caused by an electrical explosion. It was surreal, to say the least.

There was no hysteria. No crying. It was eerily quiet. I returned to the laundry room, and told my family it was safe to come out. One by one, we climbed over the tangled tree and fence, and made our way toward Main Street. Massive amounts of

trees blocked our driveway and many roadways, forcing us to climb and jump where we would normally walk.

We headed to my children's dad's house on Cushman Street. He, too, sustained major damage, but was unharmed. Russell wanted to stay with his dad while we walked the neighborhood. I hesitantly agreed. Matthew, Haley, Ally and I walked down Cushman to Gates, literally climbing through trees to pass. We were told there were elderly people that couldn't get out of the Colonial Village Apartments on State, so we headed that way to help.

We saw broken homes, homes off their foundations, homes without roofs, roofs without homes, lots of uprooted trees and signs. But before we could reach the apartment building, a first responder (a cop, I think) told us to take cover: a second tornado was predicted to hit in four minutes. We picked up the pace and headed towards home. We passed the Colonial Village apartments, unable to stop and help anyone, because we were again running for our lives.

Another warning echoed the streets: "Get inside! Tornado coming, two minutes!"

I could not keep up with Matthew and the girls. I told them to run ahead, stay together and get back in the laundry room while I got Russell. As soon as we split up, I heard the chirp of my cell phone. It was my mother calling. Hastily, I told her, "I'm running to get Russell, there's another tornado coming. We'll be hiding in the laundry room."

Grimly, I recall the reason for being so specific: in case they had to dig us out.

I finally reached my son at his dad's house, took his hand, and started running. By now, Main Street was completely deserted, except one person parked at Nothe's gas station, and a first responder who told me, "There's no time to get home, go to the town hall."

Rapid thoughts ran through my head. Town office buildings were already damaged. Did he mean old town hall? The apartment building next door to our home has a basement. We could go there. But I was worried that Matthew, Haley & Ally would possibly risk getting hurt themselves trying to find us. So, we ran for home, back the way we came. As we turned the corner into the parking lot next door, the air was gray, and the wind picked up. I had to hold my breath, squeeze my son's hand and run through a gauntlet of

slate shingles that were now coming off the roof next door. Over the tree and chain link fence, and we were back into our first floor laundry room.

We gave a little extra time for the storm to pass, so as not to be caught off guard. We emerged into a home filled with more glass and trees, a roof and rain, and no electricity. Our yard was filled with fallen trees, glass, patio furniture. Our cars were severely damaged and our motorcycles were not where we left them.

Our home was hit by a tornado on June 1, 2011. Since that day, I have not rested. The recovery process is long and convoluted. The stress caused by insurance agents and contractors can be crippling. The loss of trees and privacy is depressing. The amount of work to be done is daunting. The fear of rain and wind is persistent. I wake up tired. I go to bed sore. My marriage, which was previously solid, is now in jeopardy.

Monson. Looks. Ugly.

And now it seems we won't be able to sell our home as easily as we previously thought. I find it painfully ironic when people say there was no loss of life in the town of Monson. As I see it, the loss of life is tremendous and obvious as you drive past acres of twisted, skeletal remains of what were once strong, noble trees. We tried to spare any trees that looked promising in our own yard, but when tropical storm Irene blew through, it was clear that internal damage had been done. Eventually, we lost every single tree from our tree-lined quarter acre property.

On the last day of May, I could see one house from my back yard. One day later, I stopped counting at 35.

For one month, we walked to the First Church almost daily for food, company, information and supplies. A network of very dedicated volunteers assembled, created a Facebook page, and matched tornado victim's needs with volunteer

abilities/donations. Someone has not forgotten that we can't do this alone!

That someone goes by many names: Karen, Peter, Lenny, Clive, Charlie, Melissa, Chris, Jill, Tim, Wendy, Alison, Jo, Wayne, and countless others. Simply put, without volunteers, there would be no recovery. More simply put, "We are Monson Strong" or so I tell myself as I wipe away the tears that still fall every time I drive into town.

My daughter, Nikki, and I arrived at the Island Pond Road area and had to walk in. At first, all we saw were downed power lines but in no time, we saw homes in pieces. Roofs were completely gone. Trees rested on homes; such horror. Yet, some homes remained virtually untouched.

As we walked toward my niece, Kelly's, home, we commented on one particular street—probably the worst we'd seen so far. We kept walking until we realized we had passed her street. We turned

around. We felt shock when we realized the street that looked the worst was Kelly's street. At first we couldn't find her home; we were all turned around. Finally, we saw people we knew and that helped guide our way.

Tears streamed down our faces we saw Kelly, her husband, Jim, their daughter, Jennifer, and the family dog, Diesel—all unharmed. They took us on a tour of what

was left of their house. The roof over the kitchen and bathroom was completely gone. Windows were broken and glass was everywhere. Jennifer's bedroom had the only remaining ceiling. Their belongings were everywhere. The basement had a huge crack the whole length of the house— completely destroyed. It was just as horrible outside; devastation at its best. Their garage was one big pile. Trees lay everywhere.

Many people helped move and salvage what we could. I worked specifically in Jennifer's room, saving what I could. There was horrible a smell because only one ceiling remained and there was a lot of water damage. That day, my nephew, Tommy, and I went to the store. We bought sandwich supplies to feed everyone. My heart broke for everyone who faced this horrible time.

The next day I returned early. The attitude of gratefulness was evident all around. Kelly and Jim were more focused and their attitude was: "We are safe and we will rebuild."

Family and friends spent Thursday, Friday and Saturday salvaging what we could for them. There were no complaints; everyone worked together. We cleared the yard, emptied the garage, and moved all trash to the front yard. It was hard work, but I would do it again in a heartbeat.

We knew their house was scheduled for a demolition because the structure was unsafe. On Sunday, just days later, we all gathered for the event. Jim, Kelly and Jennifer took a final walk through of their home. Emotions were high as we all stood on the side watching, tears running down our faces. We stood with them as their house got demolished.

It took maybe ten minutes for their house to tear down, but a tornado will not stop them (or others) as they rebuild their homes. We have a community that works together, and it was evident during all that I experienced.

Tammy Chappell-Kopy
WEST SPRINGFIELD

We decided to set up our HUGE tent in the back yard to let it air out during the last week in May. We had planned a nice camping trip.

"June 1st," I said to Dave, my husband, "We need to pick up the tent. I think we are going to get a storm later."

Of course, he said, "No, not now. Later, we will."

We went inside and saw on the news there was a storm, a pretty bad one, on its way. My son, David, had done his normal routine and went upstairs to his room.

My niece, Jennifer, called me, FREAKING OUT. She kept telling me over and over that her brother told her to get down into the basement; there was a tornado. I told her he was just messing with her. She and the baby, Hunter, could go back upstairs.

She hung up. I didn't hear anything for a few minutes. The news cast said there was "tornadic" activity in Northampton. I'd never heard that word before. So we glued ourselves to the television. They showed the tornado footage.

I said, "Oh my god. That looks like it's right here!!!"

I looked out the window just as the news said, "West Springfield, Springfield, Agawam, etc take cover there is a tornado in the area."

I just happened turn and see what looked like mud flying everywhere outside. I screamed up to my son to get downstairs. I became frantic. My husband started to yell for him, too.

My son yelled down, "WHAT?"

I yelled, "TORNADO! LET'S GO!"

Dave and my son grabbed their shoes and ran down the stairs to the first floor apartment. They were pounding on the door to notify our neighbor. I was at the top of the stairs screaming my head off. I was so hysterical that, in the chaos, I forgot I'd dialed my sister, Jenn, in Ohio. My nephew answered and I didn't know it. He listened to me scream like crazy!

Then, the house began to shake. I felt like we were going to die. The skies turned a really weird bright orange color. I was paralyzed with fear until my dog, Jack, already downstairs with my husband, ran up the stairs and bit me in my side. It was as if he was shouting, "Mommy let's go."

I managed to make it down to the basement with my husband, son, and neighbor, Tom, yelling at me to run. And when I got there ... my husband and I hugged really hard. We were so scared.

After all became calm, we went upstairs.

I tried to settle down and call my family. I reached my Dad first. He said, "Get down again; there's another on coming."

Oh man; I couldn't do another.

So, we went down again. In total that day, we were up and down from the basement about four times ... until we knew we were clear.

I got in touch with my sister, Jenn. She asked if we were okay. I confirmed that we were. She explained what happened when I called. I couldn't apologize enough to my nephew, Austin, but he was actually excited that he heard a real tornado! You've got to love eleven-year-old boys, right?

Immediately after the tornado, debris was everywhere. I walked out to get into my truck, but the back window had been smashed in. The front driver's side was also shattered. It was unsafe to drive.

The next few hours were spent trying to locate family and friends. We went about a week without seeing one friend, Harold.

We had no power for three days, I believe. The only way to contact anyone was to walk to them. The streets were impassable. The only place open for business was CVS. Even Big Y was closed.

FEMA came to the rescue for lots of people. Unfortunately when I got my check for my truck, I had to use it for my rent. I lost my job three days before the tornado hit.

There are still people that come around once in a great while to make sure people are okay, which I find to be very helpful.

Toto
BRIMFIELD

At two weeks old, Toto, the kitten, was brought into the emergency operations center the day after the tornado. He was shivering, hungry and cold. The staff took care of him as best they could and turned him over to the disaster response team from the Boston Animal Rescue League. Two months later, he was adopted and given as an anniversary gift to Jonathan Hall, Brimfield Paramedic. Now, little Toto is back home in Brimfield!!

On June 1, 2011, five other people (one who is my daughter) and I were working on the second floor at our call center at 989 Main Street. About ten minutes before the tornado hit, we started to hear of the possibility of one happening. We checked the warnings that the news channel posted on its web page. We snickered at the "take cover now" part. Being from Springfield, we didn't take the warning seriously and continued to work.

Then, it got really dark. A co-worker walked over to the window and screamed that there was a Tornado coming across the bridge! We didn't believe him. After the third shout from him, I got

up to go look. I got half way down the office when I saw it: big gray, swirly, dusty, full of black spots cloud. I screamed for everyone to get downstairs. The basement door was locked and the best we could do was huddle together in the first floor hallway as far away from the windows as possible. All we could hear was the loud whistle of the wind, things hitting the windows and building, and alarms going off.

Within a few seconds the hall started to fill with white smoke. I assume it was dust and drywall. That's when I really got scared.

We were all terrified, huddled together in that hallway. It was over in about 20-25 seconds. We opened the back door, and the first thing we saw was my van. It looked like it had been blown up. The windows were completely blown out; there were pieces of lumber sticking into and on top of it. It was covered with black dirt and mud.

As we cautiously walked further outside, we started to see more devastation. A car horn was blaring. Around the corner, there was a black car with a log pierced through the roof, crushing the driver's side down so that we could not see into the car. Everyone on the street thought that the driver was still in the car and must be seriously hurt. It took a lot of yelling from everyone before someone in the crowd managed to let us know that she had gotten out safely through the passenger side and got into a building for safety.

When we went around to the front of our building, we saw lots of bricks on the sidewalk. Part of the third floor of our building was completely gone.

We all tried to call our families, but the networks were busy. It took a very long time, but I was finally able to get through to my son. I frantically told him what had happened and asked him to call my husband to come get my daughter and me. While we waited for him, we continued to walk around our building. We were scared of stepping on power lines, and there was a strong smell of gas. My daughter and I decided to get away from where all the cars were, thinking the odor was from leaking gas tanks.

That's when we saw the four-story apartment building behind us. The fourth floor was blown off. Water sprayed out of the top of it. We were afraid of what we were being sprayed with. There was a huge tree down crossing Union Street. A house had imploded—at first we couldn't tell what it was. Things were hanging from trees and houses. Cars were demolished. People walked around in shock. It didn't take long for the authorities to arrive and take action. We were asked to evacuate the area. They assumed there was a gas leak, more than likely coming from the South End Community Center, which I might add had no roof! We were told to go to the Mass Mutual Center. It was amazing to see the amount of damage on Main and Union, with no damage at all on Maple Street.

We met up with my husband and tried to make our way home. We worried about his mother.

She lives in East Forest Park, right off Plumtree Road. We'd heard the tornado went right through there. We tried to make it over there, but it was impossible. At the time, we didn't know how much damage there was on Plumtree and Island Pond Road.

After about thirty minutes, we got word that she was okay. I live in Palmer and tried to get home through Wilbraham. We had the radio on. We kept hearing warnings of more tornados touching down all over the place, Springfield, Chicopee, Ludlow, Wilbraham, Three Rivers, Palmer, Monson, etc. My daughter and I were sick to our stomachs. We begged my husband to pull over so that we could run into someone's house for safety.

We were in panic mode.

We got about halfway down Main Steet in Wilbraham when we had to turn around, due to downed trees in the middle of the road. We eventually made our way to Boston Road and finally made it home, safely.

June 2, 2011, they demolished the building I work in. We weren't allowed to go into the building to retrieve anything. My van was still in the parking lot. At first everyone, including the police, thought my van was under the rubble from our building. Eventually, I discovered that it was still there, although it was a total loss. About a month later, the insurance company was able to tow it out of there.

We are still in the process of opening a new office in Springfield, months later. It's been a slow process. In the meantime, our Springfield employees have been able to work from home. The most amazing thing about our experience of being in a tornado is that we all made it out alive and uninjured!

The windows were completely blown out; there were pieces of lumber sticking into and on top of it. It was covered with black dirt and mud.

As we cautiously walked further outside, we started to see more devastation. A car horn was blaring. Around the corner, there was a black car with a log pierced through the roof, crushing the driver's side down so that we could not see into the car. Everyone on the street thought that the driver was still in the car and must be seriously hurt. It took a lot of yelling from everyone before someone in the crowd managed to let us know that she had gotten out safely through the passenger side and into a building for safety.

When we went around to the front of our building, we saw lots of bricks on the sidewalk. Part of the third floor of our building was completely gone.

We all tried to call our families, but the networks were busy. It took a very long time, but I was finally able to get through to my son. I frantically told him what had happened and asked him to call my husband to come get my daughter and me. While we waited for him, we continued to walk around our building. We were scared of stepping on power lines, and there was a strong smell of gas. My daughter and I decided to get away from where all the cars were, thinking the odor was from leaking gas tanks.

That's when we saw the four-story apartment building behind us. The fourth floor was blown off. Water sprayed out of the top of it. We were afraid of what we were being sprayed with. There was a huge tree down crossing Union Street. A house had imploded—at first we couldn't tell

what it was. Things were hanging from trees and houses. Cars were demolished. People walked around in shock. It didn't take long for the authorities to arrive and take action. We were asked to evacuate the area. They assumed there was a gas leak, more than likely coming from the South End Community Center, which I might add had no roof! We were told to go to the Mass Mutual Center. It was amazing to see the amount of damage on Main and Union, with no damage at all on Maple Street.

We met up with my husband and tried to make our way home. We worried about his mother. She lives in East Forest Park, right off Plumtree Road. We'd heard the tornado went right through there. We tried to make it over there, but it was impossible. At the time, we didn't know how much damage there was on Plumtree and Island Pond Road.

After about thirty minutes, we got word that she was okay. I live in Palmer and tried to get home through Wilbraham. We had the radio on. We kept hearing warnings of more tornados touching down all over the place, Springfield, Chicopee, Ludlow, Wilbraham, Three Rivers, Palmer, Monson, etc. My daughter and I were sick to our stomachs. We begged my husband to pull over so that we could run into someone's house for safety.

We were in panic mode.

We got about halfway down Main Steet in Wilbraham when we had to turn around, due to downed trees in the middle of the road. We eventually made our way to Boston Road and finally made it home, safely.

June 2, 2011, they demolished the building I work in. We weren't allowed to go into the building to retrieve anything. My van was still in the parking lot. At first everyone, including the police, thought my van was under the rubble from our building. Eventually, I discovered that it was still there, although it was a total loss. About a month later, the insurance company was able to tow it out of there.

We are still in the process of opening a new office in Springfield, months later. It's been a slow process. In the meantime, our Springfield employees have been able to work from home. The most amazing thing about our experience of being in a tornado is that we all made it out alive and uninjured!

Like any great disaster, everyone has a story. We all remember where we were when the tornado struck Western Massachusetts on June 1, 2011. Many of us know someone who lost something that day; the effects were far reaching and long term. No story is more valuable or interesting than the next. And each one adds a new dimension to the experience.

This book contains only a handful of tornado stories. But it comes with the hope that we will always remember that healing takes time, continued conversations about survival must occur and never forget that tornados do occur in Massachusetts.

Thank you to everyone who contributed. This book wouldn't have been possible without you. If you'd like to comment or share your story, please visit www.SpringfieldTornados.com or join the Facebook community page. We would love to hear from you and keep the progress going.

~Loretta Kapinos & Shawn Morse

For More Information On

Visit www.AuthorMikeInk.com

Established

2010

About the Authors

Shawn Morse was raised in Western Massachusetts. When an EF3 tornado caused destruction in his community, he was inspired to help his neighbors. On June 2, 2011, he established a Facebook page to post news and updates. He plans to support rebuilding efforts and continue raising awareness through his work at www.SpringfieldTornados.com. Shawn lives in West Springfield with his girlfriend and step-daughter.

Loretta Kapinos is an Emergency Department Registered Nurse and writer. She received a Bachelor of Science at University of Massachusetts, Amherst. Her research interests include disaster response/relief and childhood development. She is currently working on a Young Adult novel. Loretta lives in Western Massachusetts with her husband and two children. For more information, find her at www.lorettajokapinos.com.

PHOTO CREDITS

www.ingramcontent.com/pod-product-compliance
Lightning Source LLC
Chambersburg PA
CBHW060812270326
41929CB00002B/15